Journey through PAKISTAN

Journey through
PAKISTAN

Mohamed Amin · Duncan Willetts
Graham Hancock

THE BODLEY HEAD
LONDON · SYDNEY
TORONTO

Acknowledgements

We would like to thank the President, the Government and the people of Pakistan for their courtesy, help and hospitality, without which this book would not have been possible. In particular our thanks go to Masood ul Rauf, Anwar Ahmad, Kafil Ahmad and Colonel Siddiq Salik for their sustained interest in the project and their useful comments on the text.

Grateful acknowledgement is also made to S.H.S. Jafri and S.M. Baqar who accompanied us on our travels.

We owe a debt of gratitude to the Frontier Works Organization of the Pakistan Army, with special thanks to Major-General Syed Shujaat Hussain; Brigadier Nazir Ahmed; and Colonel Raza Hussain Shah. Thanks are owed, too, to our helicopter pilots in the Northern Areas: Lt. Col. Kamal Khan, Captain Mohamed Ahmed Raashid, Major Kaukab Aziz Bhatti and Captain Shabab Khan, who flew a series of difficult missions amongst high mountains and through narrow rocky passes for us to photograph the Karakorams and the Himalayas. The FWO also introduced us to the Karakoram Highway, which they built and are now charged with maintaining. We pay tribute to the courage, fortitude, morale and patriotism of the engineers and soldiers who keep this dramatic road open the year round, battling against earthquakes and landslides, snow and ice.

Finally, we owe much to the unfailing support of our wives and children—Dolly and Salim Amin; Sahra, Adan, Sean and Leila Hancock—through all the months of work and the long absences from home.

First published 1982 by
The Bodley Head Ltd
9 Bow Street,
LONDON WC2E 7AL.

British Library Cataloguing in Publication Data

Amin, Mohamed

Journey through Pakistan.
1. Pakistan—Description and travel—Pictorial works
I. Title II. Willetts, Duncan III. Hancock, Graham
915.49′1045   DS377
ISBN 0–370–30489–6

© Camerapix 1982

This book was designed and produced by,

Camerapix Publishers International
P.O. Box 45048,
Nairobi, Kenya.

Design: Craig Dodd

Filmset by Keyspools Ltd, England.
Printed in Italy by Arnoldo Mondadori Editore, Verona.

Contents

Opposite: Nanga Parbat, with Astore Valley in the foreground. The western anchor of the great Himalayan Range, Nanga Parbat, stands 26,660 feet (8,125 metres) high. Nanga Parbat means 'Naked Mountain'. Not only is the mountain hard to reach but it presents formidable difficulties to the climber, with its unstable glaciers and ice terraces constantly sloughing off vast avalanches; the terrain is much worse than that of Everest, the approach route longer, and many more intermediate camps are needed for a successful ascent.

Pakistan stands at the crossroads of the world where the cultures of the Middle East and Asia meet and become one. Here ancient history exerts a profound and mellowing influence over the manner in which the technologies and attitudes of the late twentieth century are taken up, interpreted and used. Here religion and nationalism converge within society to a fine point of common feelings and shared values. Here a long ribbon of river unites disparate geographical features, tying mountains to the sea and deserts to green and fertile plains.

Pakistan is a physically dramatic country and this drama shapes and influences the everyday life of the people. It conditions their behaviour and colours their outlook on the world around them.

More than thirty million years ago the giant natural forces that shaped the continents and the oceans as we know them today raised up a great buckled arc of mountains between central Asia and the Indian land mass. These mountains—the Himalayas, the Karakorams, the Hindu Kush range and the Sulaimans—now form the northern and western borders of Pakistan. Eight of the world's ten highest peaks are to be found here, including Mount Godwin-Austen—K2—which, at 28,250 feet (8,610 metres), bows only to mighty Everest in earth's struggle to reach up to the skies.

The same natural forces that threw up the mountains around Pakistan also carved gateways into those sheer and forbidding walls. These gateways were destined to enter into human history and to inspire poets and philosophers, soldiers and kings. Most of us have probably never heard of the Kurram, Tochi, Gomal and Bolan Passes, but the Khyber, their infamous northern cousin, is a familiar name and we all have an image in our minds of the fierce and formidable tribesmen who guard it.

A sizeable minority of Pakistanis are mountain people, and their courage, dignity and independence run like bright threads through the fabric of national life. The valleys and the hillsides are the homelands of the Pathans, the world's most numerous tribal community; their harsh and unrelenting code of honour contrasts with their strangely soft and gentle lyric poetry handed down from father to son. Here too, ranged out across the roof of Pakistan, are to be found the Baluch, the Kohistanis, the pagan Kalash of the Chitral Highlands, and the Hunzakut, for centuries cut off from the mainstream of progress in a remote northern Shangri-La but now facing up to the technical explosion of the modern world with fortitude and dignity.

Overleaf: K2, 28,250 feet (8,610 metres) high, is Pakistan's highest mountain and the second highest in the world. It stands on the border between Pakistan and China. The photograph shows the southern face, from the Godwin-Austen glacier, and was taken from the open door of a helicopter flying at 17,600 feet (5,364 metres) with an outside temperature well below freezing. K2, first climbed in 1954, is also known as Mount Godwin-Austen, after a British surveyor who explored the glaciers in the region in the 1860s.

The Indus River, the other outstanding geographical feature of beautiful Pakistan, has influenced the people's outlook on life in the same way that the craggy mountains have forged the resilience of Pakistan's frontier peoples. Rising in Tibet from a spring known as 'The Mouth of the Lion', the Indus flows down through the Karakoram Mountains to enter the northern wastes of Pakistan. Thence it continues its 2,880-kilometre journey southwards and westwards through the heart of the country. At first it flows fast and tumultuously; later it becomes broad, spent and sluggish at the point where it enters the Arabian Sea near the city of Karachi.

All the way along its length the great river supports and nourishes agricultural settlements. It is in the middle ground, however, in the Pakistani provinces of Punjab and Sind, that the lifegiving virtues of the Indus and of the related river systems of the Beas, the Sutlej, the Ravi, the Chenab and the Jhelum, are most felt and most apparent. In these provinces, wheat and sugar-cane, cotton and tobacco all flourish, and people discard the rigid tribal culture of the hills in favour of a looser and more materialistic ruralism. In thousands of villages scattered amongst the fields, the orchards and the plantations, energies and ingenuity are harnessed to the soil and to the seasons. Hard work, like breathing and eating, is regarded as a natural function which no one can afford to shirk.

The same basic ethic is also to be found in towns and cities in the Indus Valley, where the business of business is business, and where the working day is long and leisure hours are short. In the teeming bazaars and busy offices one has the sense of a nation that has suddenly realized the tremendous power of its own vitality and is about to embark on an unstoppable crusade into the modern age. At the same time, however, there is a wisdom and a maturity of response which suggests that the offerings of advanced industrial society will be carefully sifted and selected, and that only the good will be kept while the bad will be discarded.

Such wisdom perhaps stems from the sense of history that nurtures Pakistani society. Like other great rivers in the Middle East and Asia—the Nile, the Tigris and the Euphrates—the mighty Indus gave birth to a remarkable civilization. At a time when the people of Europe lived in caves and dressed in animal skins, an advanced urban culture flowered in the Indus Valley, a culture which produced elaborate and skilfully-crafted artefacts, houses of burnt bricks, and well-planned drainage systems. Ruins discovered at Moenjodaro in Sind and at Harappa in the Punjab suggest that this society first emerged between 4,500 and 5,000 years ago, that it enclosed an area of land at least 1,600 kilometres long from north to south, and that, at its height, it traded with ancient Egypt and with Mesopotamia.

The Indus Valley Civilization collapsed around 1500 BC and its people vanished without trace into the mists of history. At about this time, we know, the subcontinent was invaded from the north by wild barbarian nomads from central Asia whom the historians call the Aryans. It is

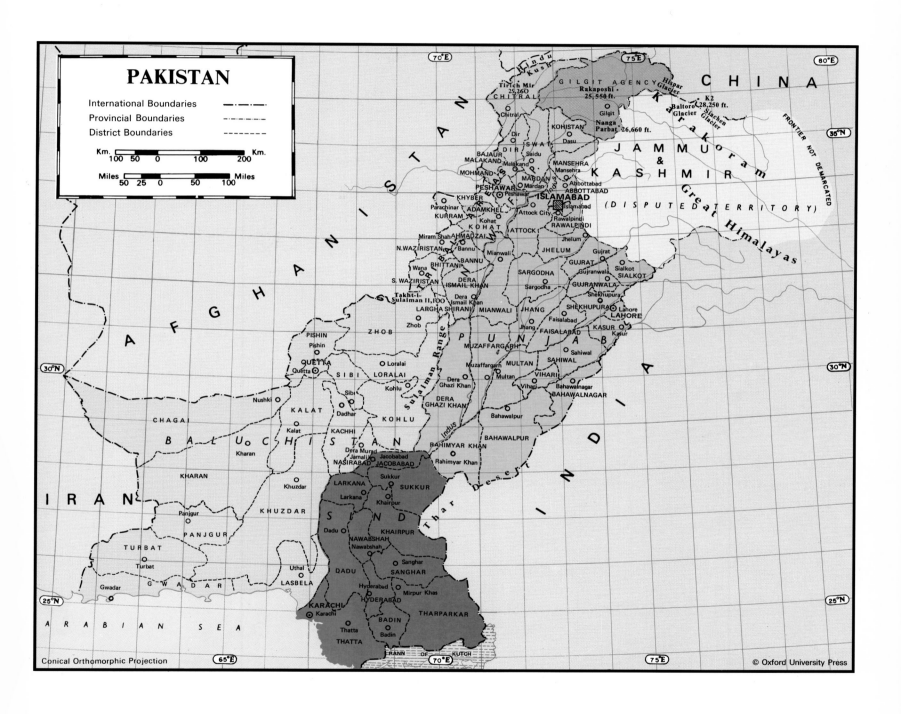

PAKISTAN

International Boundaries — · — · —
Provincial Boundaries — · · — · · —
District Boundaries — — — — —

Km. 100 50 0 100 200 Km.

Miles 50 25 0 50 100 Miles

Conical Orthomorphic Projection

© Oxford University Press

Overleaf: Dramatic ice-strewn terrain near K2 in Concodia, northern Pakistan, where several major glaciers meet at the foot of the Karakoram mountain range. Foreground is the 58-kilometre-long Baltoro Glacier. Background is Broad Peak, 26,400 feet (8,047 metres) with Gasherbrum IV, 26,000 feet (7,925 metres), in the far distance.

probable that the rich merchants of Harappa and Moenjodaro simply fled before them. It is also probable that the Aryans learned something from the cities they sacked and that they incorporated this new knowledge into their own culture, for many of them settled in the Indus Valley, cultivating the land and building permanent towns and cities of their own.

Invasions are an oft-repeated theme in the history of Pakistan. Alexander the Great led his army here in 327 BC after conquering all of Greece, Egypt and Mesopotamia, hoping to extend and enrich his short-lived Macedonian empire further. His foot-soldiers and cavalry swarmed through the Khyber Pass and along the banks of the Kabul River from Afghanistan, and made their way to the Indus. There they constructed boats and, some sailing, some marching, journeyed south to a point near modern Karachi on the Arabian Sea where they quit the subcontinent forever. They fought many battles on their route and generally outmanoeuvred and outclassed any opposition. Alexander, however, was seriously wounded in a skirmish near the town of Multan. He recovered from the injury; but the fact that his troops, having been away from their homes for ten years, were in a near-mutinous state, finally persuaded him to close the campaign. He left behind several thousand settlers but after news of his death in 323 BC filtered back to them, they too drifted away.

The hold of the Greeks in Pakistan was short-lived, and it is difficult today to find even the faintest trace of their influence. The same cannot be said of another invasion that took place just over one thousand years after Alexander's death. In AD 711 Mohamed Bin Qasim, a brilliant 19-year-old Arab general from Basra (in modern Iraq), marched into Pakistan by way of Persia and the Baluchistan coast at the head of an army of 6,000 men. Employing a method of warfare never before seen in the subcontinent—large carriage-drawn catapults capable of hurling heavy stone missiles across distances of about 200 yards (183 metres)—Mohamed Bin Qasim stormed and captured the port of Debul (near modern Bhanbore). From there he marched north to Nerun (Hyderabad) where he engaged Raja Dahir, the local Hindu ruler, in battle. Dahir had 20,000 infantry and 5,000 cavalry and apparently took the field himself seated on an elephant in the company of two concubines, one supplying him with arrows as fast as he could shoot and the other feeding him with betel nuts. Mohamed Bin Qasim defeated him with contemptuous ease and Dahir was killed in the affray.

Above: Silver coin depicts Alexander the Great, the Greek general who led his army through Pakistan in the fourth century BC. It was minted by another Greek ruler, Agathokles, in the second century BC.

From Nerun the Arab army continued its relentless northward march until it arrived at Multan. There, with effective control over the whole of Sind and a fair part of the Punjab as well, Mohamed Bin Qasim called a halt and set about consolidating his rule and strengthening his hold over the people. Fate did not allow him to see this task completed. Two years after his arrival in Multan he somehow displeased the all-powerful Caliph of Baghdad and was recalled and executed. No one knows for certain exactly how Mohamed Bin Qasim incurred the Caliph's anger, and there are several different accounts of the manner of his death. Probably he achieved too much too quickly and too visibly.

Certainly there can be no doubting the scale of Mohamed Bin Qasim's achievement, which, in a sense, has shaped all the subsequent history of Pakistan. In administering the territories he conquered, he planted the seeds of a new social order which was characterized by a spirit of tolerance and conciliation, and an assertion of the equality of all human beings in the eyes of God. However, his real importance lies in his rôle as the bringer of Islam to Pakistan—and, indeed, whatever social and political arrangements he may have made were products of the pure evangelistic desert faith to which he adhered.

Islam is by far the most important of all the influences at work in Pakistan today. Its hold over the hearts and minds of the people is immense; it inspires a mood of unity and national purpose amongst disparate ethnic groups and between widely separated economic strata; as a world religion it draws Pakistan into the broad currents of international affairs; as an ethical system it has set in motion a radical process of rethinking and restructuring within society.

Mohamed Bin Qasim came to Sind with a sword in his hand but Islam, then less than a century old, took root there through genuine intellectual and spiritual conversions rather than through forceful persuasion. In the centuries that followed, the subcontinent was invaded repeatedly by Muslim armies. Turks, Afghans and Mongols poured through the northern passes to sack the rich cities of the south and plunder the fertile agricultural plains. Some of the invaders, like Mohamed Bin Qasim, were tolerant of other faiths and, by following the true Islamic creed that there should be 'no coercion in religion', won converts by their own example. Others, like the Amir Timur, Timurlane, (who was said to have built towers of the severed heads of his enemies) were less patient. Slowly but surely, however, Islam spread outwards from Sind to encompass all the lands that now make up Pakistan. Soldiers played their part in this process, but equally

16

important were the saints and holy men who ventured into the mountain strongholds where no army could force its way, and across the desert wastes in which no general was interested. Today, the soldiers have passed into obscurity but the saints are still remembered and revered by the ordinary people who, through the length and breadth of the country, have erected shrines to their memory.

Some 800 years after the death of Mohamed Bin Qasim, the turbulent history of the subcontinent, and of the many competing dynasties that struggled for ascendancy there, gave way to a period of political calm and cultural achievement that was to last for more than three centuries.

This period began in 1525, when a Turkish chief named Babur followed the same road of conquest into India that so many warlords had taken before him. In 1526, at Panipat, 80 kilometres from Delhi, he defeated the ruler, Ibrahim Lodhi, in battle. In the following year another major battle was fought and won, and the year after that another. By 1530, when he died, Babur controlled an empire that stretched from Kabul in Afghanistan through the Punjab to the borders of Bengal.

Babur founded the Mughal dynasty. His personality, and the personalities of the five other Great Mughals who followed him, are stamped upon the face of modern Pakistan with indelible firmness. As historian Percival Spear has written, 'The Mughals rose above the general run of kings and princes; they had a divine right, a something which set them apart from all others.' So powerful was this rare, intangible quality adhering to the Mughal throne that a hundred years after its loss of effective control over the subcontinent, loyalty to the dynasty was a factor in the Mutiny of 1857 that saw Hindu and Muslim alike join hands to rise up against the British Empire.

The Mughals were great builders. Any traveller in Pakistan visiting the monuments, mosques and palaces today that they left behind can see the special creative talent that the emperors possessed in addition to their military prowess and administrative genius.

Babur, the father of the dynasty, was first and foremost a brilliant soldier; but he was also a poet of great sensitivity and a lover of gardens and fountains. There was nothing of the ruthless tyrant in his nature. His memoirs suggest a man who was able to combine ambition with humility and gentleness of manner with firm reasoning.

Right: Near Gilgit, in Pakistan's rugged northern areas, farmers use techniques of intensive cultivation to win a year-round living from thin ribbons of fertile land lining the rushing mountain rivers. The terrain is divided into a series of isolated but densely-populated valleys that, in years gone by, nurtured many self-contained kingdoms—such as Hunza, Nagar and Yasin—with their own unique cultures and ways of life.

Right: A girl of the Baluch tribe, which claims an ancient Semitic lineage and traces its origins back 4,000 years to Aleppo in Syria, from where they migrated slowly eastwards.

Below: Kalash girl wearing a traditional shell head-dress. The Kalash are a pagan people and live in three remote valleys in north-west Pakistan.

Below: Camel-train near the Kurrum River on the road to Parachinar in the North-West Frontier Province. The camel is the universal beast of burden in the Frontier areas.

Left: Punjabi farmer. Village life in the Punjab is simple and uncluttered, but prosperous.

Opposite right: Pathan elder. Old people in Pakistan are revered for their wisdom and have an honoured place in society.

Opposite left: Splendidly-attired tribesman, a member of the Khyber Rifles contingent guarding Pakistan's border with Afghanistan.

Left: The Karakoram mountain range in northern Pakistan near the border with China contains some of the most dramatic mountain scenery in the world. Peaks higher than 18,000 feet (5,486 metres) are commonplace and many remain unconquered by climbers. Cocksill, remarkable for its pyramid-like shape, dominates the Karokoram Highway near the 15,072 foot (4,593 metres) Khunjerab Pass.

Babur's son Humayun inherited much of his father's sensitivity but he did not have the same qualities of decisive statesmanship or the same quick military skills. His reign was marred by internecine strife and he suffered a lengthy period of exile. He did eventually overcome his enemies and, in 1555, he won his way back to Delhi. It is a comment on a man who was always a better scholar than soldier that, when he died just six months later, it was not on the battlefield but from a fall in his observatory.

Humayun's son Akbar was just fourteen years old when he took the throne in 1556. His survival in the early years owed much to the loyalty of Bairam Khan, the tutor and regent that his father had appointed to care for him. However, as the boy-king's power and authority grew, it became apparent that he was going to become a wise and enlightened leader, quite able to survive the rough-and-tumble of political in-fighting, and that his qualities of statesmanship, combined with skill in the battlefield, had prepared him for a great rôle in life.

Akbar assumed direct rule in 1560, at the age of eighteen, and, during the next forty-five years, extended the frontiers of the Mughal Empire to the Bay of Bengal in the east and the Persian border with Afghanistan in the north-west. He also held dominion over much of southern India, over Kashmir, and over Baluchistan and Sind.

Akbar started his imperial career as a devout Muslim, but died something of a heretic. He was extremely tolerant of other faiths; in 1562 he abolished most of the restrictions on the Hindus and, in 1579, he lifted the *Jaziya*, a tax that had hitherto been imposed on all non-Muslims. However, he allowed a cult to develop around his personality, and his apparent wish that this cult should become the basis of a 'universal religion', embracing the best features of all the other faiths of the empire, caused him to fall seriously out of line with his Islamic advisers.

Akbar called his personal creed *Din Illahi*—'the divine faith'. It did have a brief rôle in the dynamics and administration of his empire, welding together a secular state out of the variety of cultures, traditions, religions and peoples that made up the subcontinent; but it attracted few genuine adherents and faded away when Akbar died. Looking back on Akbar's reign, Muslims today prefer to remember him for his gigantic military conquests and for the way in which he encouraged artistic and cultural endeavour. Many of the most prominent scholars of his time were attached to his court and benefited from his patronage.

Overleaf: High up in the picturesque Swat Valley in north-west Pakistan, the scenery rivals anything that the Swiss Alps have to offer. Towering mountains cloaked in perennial snow rise above the treeline to pierce the clouds.

On his death in 1605, after a long reign, Akbar was succeeded by his son Jehangir, one of the most attractive characters amongst the Great Mughals. The victim of a tragic love affair in his youth, Jehangir took a number of wives in later life and was described as 'a kind father, a loving husband and a benefactor to his kinsmen'. Although he had a weakness for strong drink, Jehangir built a reputation during his twenty-three years on the throne as a great and just king, and was particularly admired for his sense of fair play and for his unbiased judgements in disputes.

Jehangir died in 1628 leaving two potential heirs—his son Shah Jehan, and his stepson Shahryar. Shah Jehan took the throne and mercilessly killed Shahryar and all other possible claimants. Despite this bloody start he was to prove a good ruler.

Like other Mughals Shah Jehan was a significant patron of the arts and of architecture. In India he built the Red Fort in Delhi and, in memory of his wife Mumtaz Mahal, the Taj Mahal at Agra, one of the most beautiful buildings in the world. His legacy to modern Pakistan includes the remarkable Shalimar Gardens in Lahore and the Shish Mahal (the Hall of Mirrors) in Lahore Fort, which was built as the official residence of the Empress. Another of his buildings, the Shah Jehan Mosque in Thatta, is graced by sweeping arches and domes and contains the most elaborate display of tilework in the subcontinent.

Above: Centuries-old illuminated Quranic scroll testifies to Pakistan's Islamic belief. The faith came to Pakistan in the years soon after the death of the Prophet Muhammad.

Right: At Mansura, near Hyderabad, the site of one of the oldest mosques in South Asia stands open to the sky amidst more recent shrines and graves. The mosque was built by the Arab invaders who conquered Sind and parts of the southern Punjab in the first half of the eighth century. The remains of the pillars that supported the prayer hall can still be seen, as can the qiblah, the semi-circular niche in the foreground where the Imam stood to lead the prayers.

Opposite: The Emperor Shah Jehan with his sons. Shah Jehan's reign, the zenith of Mughal rule, lasted from 1628 until 1658. Late in life he was overthrown by his son Aurangzeb.

Shah Jehan's reign was the zenith of the Mughal era. He ruled a massive and prosperous empire and the economic surpluses it generated helped to finance the artistic achievements that he handed down to posterity. During his twenty-two years on the throne he also initiated a return to Islamic orthodoxy and to the Shariah, abolishing many of the lax practices that had been permitted by his father and grandfather.

History, however, has a way of repeating itself. Shah Jehan came to power with a sword in his hand and murdered close relatives whom he regarded as his rivals. So it seems somehow appropriate that he, in his turn, was overthrown by the sword and by the lust for power of his own children. Late in his life his four sons fought over the succession and, in 1658, Shah Jehan was deposed by the victor, Aurangzeb. Two of Aurangzeb's brothers, Dara Shikoh and Murad, were put to death while a third, Shuja, disappeared without trace. Shah Jehan was locked away in the fort at Agra with nothing but a view of his beautiful Taj Mahal to comfort him and remind him of his past glories.

Aurangzeb ruled the empire with an iron hand. He was austere and puritanical in his personal habits and an orthodox Muslim in his beliefs. He continued and strengthened the return to Islamic law that had been instituted by his father and appointed a commission of scholars to compile a code of Islamic Jurisprudence relevant to the conditions of life at that time.

Of all the Mughals, Aurangzeb came the closest to achieving the ideal of a true Islamic state in India. He also overcame a number of uprisings in the empire during his long rule and successfully extended its borders to encompass Afghanistan and the entire subcontinent. His campaigns stretched from the hills of the north-west to the plains of the Deccan, and all were conducted with the same ruthless efficiency. One of his enemies observed before conceding defeat, 'To fight against Aurangzeb is to fight against one's own destiny.'

Aurangzeb's strict interpretation of religion meant that he displayed little of the wide-ranging interest in the arts that had so absorbed his predecessors. Indeed, he believed that an excess of music and poetry would emasculate Muslim society. Nevertheless, he did leave behind some architectural splendours, most notably the Badshahi Mosque in Lahore, which has the largest courtyard of any mosque in the world.

Aurangzeb died in 1707. The forces that he had suppressed within the empire did not take long to reassert themselves. His son and successor, Bahadur Shah, was already old when he took the throne,

Above: Finely-detailed miniature paintings were a speciality of the Mughal period. This one depicts Akbar, the third Mughal emperor, who was a wise and enlightened leader and extended the frontiers of Mughal rule to the Bay of Bengal in the east and to the Persian border in the north-west. His rule lasted from 1556 until 1605.

Below: The Emperor Aurangzeb depicted reading the Holy Quran in a boat. Aurangzeb ruled the Mughal empire from 1658 until his death in 1707. He was a purist and enforced a return to strict Islamic law. One enemy observed, before conceding defeat in battle, that to fight against Aurangzeb was to fight against one's destiny.

and was confronted with one rebellion after another. He died in 1712, a dissatisfied man who had witnessed the beginning of the end of the empire founded by Babur. Though the Mughals continued to hold nominal power in at least some parts of India until the 1850s they never regained the dignity and authority of their early days and often disgraced themselves by their bad behaviour, spiritual weakness and love of intrigue. A measure of this pattern of decline is to be found in the fact that in the century following the death of Aurangzeb no less than fifteen kings ascended the Mughal throne as against the six Great Mughals of the previous 181 years.

The decline of the Mughals allowed new influences to come into play in the subcontinent. The Persian Nadir Shah was able to sack Delhi in

1739 and, in 1756, Ahmed Shah Abdali, the Afghan King of Kabul, did the same. In the latter half of the eighteenth century the Sikhs emerged as a power to be reckoned with in the Punjab. And at about the same time, the British began to extend their influence, first insidiously but soon with overwhelming military force, so that by the mid-nineteenth century, they were the new emperors of all India.

Attempts to consolidate British rule met with considerable resistance, the high point of which was the 1857 Mutiny. After the uprising was crushed, however, the Muslims—who had always been in a minority in the subcontinent, even at the height of their powers—became the victims of severe political repression and adverse discrimination. Official policy divested them of much that they owned and favoured Hindus and members of other religions for all Civil Service positions. In the newly reorganized army, too, Muslims were overlooked and pride of place was given to the Sikhs—who had not participated in the Mutiny.

As a result of Muslim misery and humiliation in India at this time, the political movement that was to preside over the creation of Pakistan almost a century later was born. In those early days, however, the idea of a separate Muslim state in the subcontinent had not even been mooted. Instead, a few gifted intellectuals set themselves the limited goal of winning constitutional rights for Muslims and safeguarding their interests.

The key figure in the aftermath of the 1857 uprising was Sir Syed Ahmed Khan, a scholar and a man of vision who, because he had not associated himself with the Mutiny, was able to wield influence with the British to an extent that other potential leaders were not. In 1875 his efforts led to the setting up of the Mohammedan Anglo-Oriental College in Aligarh which, in due course, developed into the Aligarh Muslim University. Sir Syed hoped that Aligarh would provide a focus for cultural and scientific advance amongst Muslims and that from it an educated cadre of leaders would emerge.

He was a realist, and this realism led him to think of Muslims and Hindus, without acrimony or any sense of prejudice, not just as two peoples of different faiths but actually as two distinct and separate nations. 'If the English should leave India,' he asked, 'then who would be the country's rulers? Our two nations, the Mohammedan and the Hindu, could not sit on the same throne and be equal in power. It is necessary that one of them should conquer the other and throw it down. To hope that both could remain equal is to desire the impossible and the inconceivable.' In another speech he reiterated this view: 'I am fully convinced that the two nations would not be able to participate wholeheartedly in any activity whatsoever.'

Left: Quaid-i-Azam Mohammad Ali Jinnah, the founder of Pakistan, without whose leadership in the 1930s and 1940s Pakistan would never have been created as an independent state. 'We are a nation,' he affirmed three years before the birth of Pakistan, 'with our own distinctive culture and civilization, language and literature, art and architecture, names and nomenclature, sense of values and proportion . . . We have our own distinctive outlook on life.'

The logical outcome of thinking of this sort came in 1905 when the All-India Muslim League was established as a political organization intended to advocate and advance Muslim views. Though its initial objectives were extremely mild, the League became increasingly disenchanted with both the British Government and the Indian National Congress, the party that represented the interests of the Hindus. Great efforts were made to set up a common front against British rule. Congress, however, refused to countenance the notion of special safeguards for the Muslims of India after Independence, and, by 1928, the two parties were moving on obviously divergent tracks.

The first thirty years of the twentieth century were an exciting and momentous period for the Muslims of the subcontinent. During this time they emerged from relative obscurity to a new political consciousness and to an awareness of their own potential as a community. In this sudden awakening a number of figures stand out as being of pre-eminent importance. Foremost amongst them was a brilliant Karachi-born barrister, Mohammad Ali Jinnah, now recognized as the founder of the Pakistan nation. Dr Muhammad Iqbal, a great Islamic poet, also played a crucial and formative rôle.

In 1930, in his capacity as President of the Muslim League, Iqbal was the first man to use a political platform to launch the concept of a separate Muslim homeland in the subcontinent. Speaking at the League's Allahabad session he won the approval of the delegates when he said, 'I would like to see the Punjab, North-West Frontier Province, Sind and Baluchistan amalgamated into a single state. Self-government within the British Empire or without the British Empire, the formation of a consolidated North-West Indian Muslim state, appears to me to be the final destiny of the Muslims, at least of North-West India.'

During the 1920s Mohammad Ali Jinnah had striven with all his considerable powers to resolve the differences between the Congress and the Muslim League. In the 1930s, however, a number of bitter experiences gradually brought him round to Dr Iqbal's more radical view. In 1940 he was instrumental in getting the League formally to adopt Iqbal's vision of a separate state for Muslims. A year later, Jinnah summed up the implications of this vision with his customary eloquence: 'The ideology of the Muslim League is based on the fundamental principle that the Muslims of India are an independent nationality and any attempt to get them to merge their national and

Above: Dr Muhammad Iqbal, the Islamic poet who played such a vital rôle in the birth of Pakistan, was the first to advocate the formation of an independent Muslim state for the subcontinent.

political identity and unity will not only be resisted but, in my opinion, it will be futile for anyone to attempt it. We are determined, and let there be no mistake about it, to establish the status of an independent nation and an independent State in this subcontinent.'

The Muslims were as anxious as the rest of the population of India to secure independence from Britain, but their greatest concern was to ensure that this independence would be meaningful to them. They were no longer willing even to consider autonomy within a united India

Above: The Residency at Ziarat in Baluchistan where Quaid-i-Azam spent the last days of his life. In the foreground is Toti Khan, the chowkidar who served here during the week before the dying Quaid was flown to his residence in Karachi.

under the majority rule of the Hindu-dominated Congress party. Accordingly, while the Congress called on the British to 'Quit India', Jinnah and the Muslim League insisted that Britain should 'Divide and then Quit'.

When the Second World War ended, both the Congress Party and the Muslim League intensified their political pressure on the British Government. The League made it clear that it wanted India's six Muslim provinces—the Punjab, North-West Frontier Province, Baluchistan, Sind, Bengal and Assam—to be grouped together into an effectively self-governing Pakistan prior to Independence. The British, however, attempted to impose an interim government on India that did not fully recognize the Muslim demands, and the League therefore refused to participate.

A 'Direct Action Day' was declared on 16 August 1946, intended to explain to the public why the interim proposals were not acceptable. Although most of the demonstrations held on that day passed off peacefully enough, there was a major disaster in Calcutta when, at the instigation of the Congress Party, Hindus attempted to stop a Muslim march. More than 5,000 people lost their lives in a single afternoon and at least 10,000 were injured. Thereafter, rioting broke out over the whole of northern India, with particularly serious violence against Muslims in Bihar and Punjab.

Britain was compelled to act and to act quickly. The new Viceroy, Lord Mountbatten, initially intended Independence to be granted to the subcontinent in June 1948; however, more rioting, almost on the level of a civil war, forced him to revise the timescale. On 3 June 1947 Mountbatten announced that India would be partitioned into two independent states, India and Pakistan. The formal handover of power in Pakistan took place on 14 August 1947, with Mohammad Ali Jinnah as the Governor-General of the new State.

Pakistan—the name means 'Country of the Pure'—was born in bloodshed and turmoil and, in the early years, it only survived because of the tremendous sacrifices made by its people. In spite of the burden of several million refugees, and the untold suffering and disruption of the months immediately after Partition, when more than one million people lost their lives, the nation proved its resilience. The memory of this tragic period is still very evident amongst Pakistanis today, and is a factor in the country's strong sense of nationhood.

During the early and difficult months of Pakistan's emergence, Mohammad Ali Jinnah, although in ill-health and over seventy years of age, undertook a countrywide tour aimed at building confidence and

Above: Tomb of Dr Muhammad Iqbal outside Badshahi Mosque, facing Lahore Fort's Alamgiri Gate. He died on 21 April 1938.

Overleaf: Verdant lawn and cricket pitch in front of the Islamia College at Peshawar, one of the earliest educational institutions on the frontier. The college was built during the 1920s, and is now part of Peshawar University, which offers advanced courses in the sciences and mathematics as well as more traditional subjects like literature, languages and history.

raising people's spirits. 'Do not be overwhelmed by the enormity of the task,' he said in a speech at Lahore. 'There is many an example in history of young nations building themselves up by sheer determination and force of character. You are made of sterling material and are second to none. Keep up your morale. Do not be afraid of death. We should face it bravely to save the honour of Pakistan and of Islam. Do your duty and have faith in Pakistan. It has come to stay.'

Jinnah's rôle in this Pakistan that had indeed come to stay is immeasurable. His people bestowed upon him the title Quaid-i-Azam, 'Great Leader', because, without him, Pakistan would not have existed at all. His leadership of the Muslims of India through the 1930s and the crucial years immediately preceding Partition gave shape to their dreams and put their aspirations into a realistic and meaningful framework. One of his great gifts as a politician was that whenever he defined Pakistan he did so in terms that the man in the street could understand, and he avoided abstract philosophical principles: 'We are a nation,' he affirmed, three years before the birth of Pakistan, 'with our own distinctive culture and civilization, language and literature, art and architecture, names and nomenclature, sense of values and proportion, legal laws and moral codes, customs and calendar, history and tradition, aptitude and ambitions—in short, we have our own distinctive outlook on life.' As his biographer, Professor Ziauddin Ahmad, has commented of Quaid-i-Azam, 'When he defined Muslim nationhood in such tangible terms, every Muslim found himself testifying to the justice of this claim, and subscribing to the logical corollary of the fact and recognition of separate Muslim nationhood, viz., the demand for a Muslim homeland.'

Quaid-i-Azam Mohammad Ali Jinnah died on 11 September 1948, just thirteen months after the Muslims of India had come into their homeland. In the years since then, Pakistan has gone through many of the traumas of new nationhood, the most devastating of which was the war with India in 1971 and the formation of Bangladesh as a separate state. More recently, the Soviet invasion of Afghanistan has driven more than two million refugees into camps in north-west Pakistan and in Baluchistan, imposing a huge burden on the economy and on social services. The nation has weathered all these storms and gone on to forge a measure of prosperity in an atmosphere of unbowed optimism and hope. That it has done so owes much to the spiritual and political legacy of the early leaders and thinkers like Mohammad Ali Jinnah and Dr Muhammad Iqbal, and to the resilience and fundamental value of the Pakistan ideal that they forged.

Modern Pakistan is a country with a population of eighty-four million and a Gross National Product in excess of US $20 billion. It has a broadly-based and rapidly-expanding economy. The agricultural sector, including forestry and fishing, is the largest single source of employment for Pakistanis. The nation's food production is concentrated in the well-irrigated Indus Valley, particularly in the Punjab where almost 75 per cent of the land-area planted to wheat and rice can be found. Wheat and rice are the principal food crops and rice is also one of the largest earners of foreign exchange amongst the visible exports. Cotton is the principal non-food crop. Over two million acres, again mainly in the Punjab, are planted to cotton, which provides the raw material for Pakistan's 174 textile mills.

The production of textiles is the country's most important industry. The manufacture of cigarettes from locally-grown tobacco is also significant, as is the production of hydrogenated vegetable oil, the refining of sugar and the production of fertilizers. Cement production is on the increase and the country hopes to become a major producer of steel following the commissioning of the Pakistan Steel mill in Karachi. The country's oil-refining capacity is around 90,000 barrels per day, although most of the crude refined is at present imported.

Oil was first discovered in Pakistan in 1915 and although production has remained small (around 10,500 barrels per day, or 9 per cent of the country's requirements) a number of new wells have recently come on stream. Natural gas production is also on the increase, averaging around 850 million cubic feet per day. Most of the natural gas fields so far discovered are in Baluchistan.

Pakistan's energy needs are very considerable and are projected to grow over the coming years as the economy expands and modernizes. According to official estimates, even if a significant proportion of the nation's gas, oil and coal is harnessed for power production along with hydroelectricity, which provides around a quarter of commercial energy, the maximum installed capacity possible by the turn of the century will be only 11,000 MW. The demand for electricity at that time is likely to be in excess of 27,000 MW, an alarming difference. Because the availability of electricity is essential for economic growth, and because of the rising cost of imported oil, Pakistan has launched its own nuclear-power programme. The Director of the Pakistan Atomic Energy Commission has observed, 'Nuclear energy . . . offers the only economical and practical answer to our problem of energy shortage.' The country currently has one small 137 MW nuclear-power plant in operation in Karachi and a second plant, 600 MW, is due to be commissioned at Chashma in the Punjab's Mianwali District.

Left: The Minar-e-Pakistan in Lahore symbolizes the spirit of the Pakistan Resolution of 1940, and the call for an independent country for Muslims.

Opposite: In the cool of morning, lessons are held outdoors at Chaman in Baluchistan, near Pakistan's border with Afghanistan.

Left: Schooling tomorrow's generation in the frontier town of Miranshah. Girls are taught separately from boys but Pakistan decrees both should have equal access to education.

Pakistan has developed considerable expertise in nuclear technology, which its scientists have applied outside the energy sector to both agriculture and medicine. Three nuclear agriculture research centres have been established, at Faisalabad, at Tarnab near Peshawar, and at Tandojam, all with the task of developing new high-yielding and disease-resistant crops such as wheat, rice, cotton and pulses. Other objects of the research programme include the development of more economic storage of food grains by disinfestation through nuclear irradiation, more efficient use of water and fertilizer, and the control of insects through irradiation. The nuclear agriculture centre at Faisalabad has evolved a new high-yielding rice, dubbed Kashmir Basmati, which matures three weeks earlier than the parent variety. Since it matures earlier it therefore escapes the onset of winter and can be grown in hilly areas. The Tandojam Centre has developed a rust-resistant variety of wheat and a blight-resistant strain of potato.

The medical uses of irradiation have for some time been the subject of study at five centres, located in Karachi, Lahore, Multan, Jamshoro and Peshawar. The newest and largest nuclear medical centre is in the capital Islamabad. When complete its modern facilities will include a linear accelerator which is used for the diagnosis and treatment of both superficial and deep-seated tumours.

Pakistan may be a developing country, but its innovative approach to economic development and the vigour, intelligence and willingness to work of its people all augur well for the future. In this context one of the most important changes of recent years has been the decision that, so far as is possible, the future development of the economy should be guided by Islamic principles. Amongst other things this has meant an attempt to introduce interest-free banking in Pakistan, and to collect the *Zakat*, a nominal welfare tax prescribed by Islam, in a systematic and orderly way.

The challenge and the difficulties inherent in the Islamization of the Pakistan economy have been summed up by the Government's Committee on Islamization: 'The Islamic world, including Pakistan, is passing through the pangs of a rebirth. Not a pursuit of something new, the Islamic resurgence is the process of *rediscovering* the truth of the Islamic message in the modern world, which is by no means very receptive to this historic "event". It is not only an opportunity to "realign" ourselves—both as individuals and as a nation—with the reality of Islam. This is also a challenge to the ingenuity of the Muslim philosophers and social scientists: for while the truth of the Divine Message is immaculate and immutable, ways and means must be found to "accommodate" it within the strait-jacket of pre-existing institutions.

Above: Sunflower farm near Multan. The flowers are grown commercially for their seeds and oil.

Overleaf: In the mountain country of northern Pakistan every inch of cultivable land is brought under the plough through the use of steep terracing.

Opposite: Ploughing rice paddy in the fertile Vale of Peshawar, a farmer uses centuries-old agricultural techniques. Patiently wheeling and turning, the bullocks draw a heavy wooden plough through the deep cloying mud.

Above: Symbol of progress, the Tarbela Dam—the largest earth-filled dam in the world—is 469 feet (143 metres) high and 2,264 feet (800 metres) thick at the base. It has created a reservoir more than 80 kilometres long that provides drinking water and hydro-electric power for Islamabad and Rawalpindi.

True, the institutions will also change under the impact of Islamic reform, but that takes time. A beginning has to be made and at this stage the institutional constraints are binding. The "point of contact" of the Islamization process will be the present socio-economic set-up, which, being a hard "reality", cannot be ignored.'

Islam is a complete system governing human behaviour and belief. In Dr Muhammad Iqbal's words it is 'a state conceived as a contractual organism and animated by an ethical ideal.' One of the most important ways in which Islam impinges on economic development is the attitude towards private property. In the Islamic perspective, all wealth belongs to Allah: 'Unto Allah belongeth whatever is in the heaven and whatsoever is in the earth.' Man is, therefore, only a trustee of whatever he has and not its owner: 'and spend whereof He hath made you trustees.' As the Committee on Islamization observes, 'The Islamic position is unique and can easily be distinguished from the position of capitalism where the private ownership of wealth is a sacred institution to be preserved at all cost, as well as from the position of socialism where all wealth belongs to the State. It should be clear that, because of the concept of trusteeship, the right to private property in Islam gets vastly qualified, limiting severely the sphere of ownership itself. There is complete unanimity among Muslim scholars that such things as grazing-lands, natural forests and water resources, mines, roads, graveyards and places of congregational prayers, cannot be privately owned. As for land, ownership rights are liable to be lost if such land lies unreclaimed or is not used for three consecutive years.'

In the context of the economic system that Pakistan has inherited, the process of Islamization is a revolutionary one. It has implications not only on private property but on every form of economic activity and human endeavour. As with the Islamization of the legal system, also currently under way, it is clear that a monumental effort will be required if Pakistan is to achieve the goals that it has set itself. Inevitably, and particularly in the early days, the Government's rôle will have to be a large one. To quote again from the Committee on Islamization: 'The Islamic system, with its heavy emphasis on the act of "giving" as the essence of a just socio-economic ordering, must, to reflect God's intention, devise ways and means of checking individual greed so that all members of the society get a minimum of sustenance. Hence, to introduce Islamic reform in a country like Pakistan, the structure of which has been raised on capitalistic principles, it will be essential for the State to take up increasing responsibilities to ensure the satisfaction of the society's demand for such "basic needs" as health, education and housing.'

In Pakistan today one has the sense not of a new nation but rather of an old nation that is rediscovering itself. Islam is the beginning, the end and the middle of Pakistan's existence and it is appropriate that in the process of rediscovery it should come to occupy a paramount place in national affairs. If the people of Pakistan display a healthy self-respect, sense of purpose and confidence in their manner of living, as well as a mature tolerance of the idiosyncrasies of others, it is because they have no doubts about their own identity, an identity that is rooted and grounded in Islam. 'We are Muslims,' wrote Dr Iqbal, 'and we are compatriots to the whole world.'

Opposite: High and steep, Niltar Valley, near Gilgit, is run through with a chain of small lakes and streams that, from the air, look like emerald and turquoise gem stones.

Overleaf: The 56-kilometre-long Khyber Pass gives access to the rich and fertile Indus Valley. Often used by armies seeking to invade the subcontinent, Alexander the Great, Genghis Khan, Timurlane and Babur all came this way. Today the Pass is an important conduit for frontier trade as brightly painted lorries groan and squeal up its steep inclines and tight, hairpin bends.

Chapter Two The Magic of the Frontier

Pakistan's northern and western borders with China and Afghanistan are marked out by rugged hills and mountains ranging in height from 2,000 feet (609 metres) in the south-west to over 28,000 feet (8,535 metres) in the far north. The gateways through this otherwise unbroken barrier are occasional natural passes. By far the best-known of these is the Khyber Pass, which is 56 kilometres long, 40 kilometres being in Pakistan and the remainder in Afghanistan. From the Khyber border post at Torkham, where an old sign warns hitch-hikers that under no circumstances should they spend the night in the open in the Pass, it is a 55-kilometre journey to the city of Peshawar. Pakistan's capital, Islamabad, is 227 kilometres away, Lahore 497 kilometres, and the port of Karachi 1,782 kilometres.

Since ancient times the Khyber has formed a vital route for overland trade between Pakistan and Afghanistan, and a point of entry to the subcontinent for invading armies. Its military importance is easily explained. It is wide enough to allow troops and cavalry to march through it in disciplined ranks and its highest point, Landi Kotal, is only 3,500 feet (1,067 metres) above sea-level. Beyond the Pass, beckoning enticingly to the greedy and the bold, lies the lush Vale of Peshawar at the head of the rich and fertile Indus Valley.

In the fourth century BC, when Alexander the Great of Macedon invaded the Punjab, one of his divisions came through the Khyber. In the tenth century AD Sabuktigin, who founded the Ghaznivid dynasty, and his more famous son Mahmud, brought their armies through the Pass on their way to the conquest of much of Pakistan and northern India. There is evidence that Genghis Khan and Timurlane made use of the Pass in the thirteenth and fourteenth centuries. Babur, the first of the Mughals, also took this route on his march down into the subcontinent from Afghanistan in 1525. Rather more than 200 years later the Turk Nadir Shah came the same way during the sunset of Mughal rule.

What may at first be surprising is that more of the subcontinent's invaders did not use the Khyber Pass and that those who used it once rarely did so again. The explanation, however, is to be found in the warlike nature of the Afridi tribesmen who have lived in the Pass for millennia and have often made war or extracted tolls from those who have tried to use it as a thoroughfare. The Greek historian Herodotus, who wrote in the fifth century BC, knew them as the Aparutai and commented on their bravery. Many others since then have noted their readiness to fight. Sir Robert Warburton, a British army-officer who spent several years with the garrisons in the Khyber in the late nineteenth century, had this to say of them: 'The Afridi lad from his earliest childhood is taught by the circumstances of his existence and life to distrust all mankind, and very often his near relations, heirs to his small plot of land by right of inheritance, are his deadliest enemies.

Opposite: A crowded steam train pulls into Landi Kotal, the highest point in the Khyber Pass and end of the line for the weekly passenger service. The journey from Peshawar takes six hours.

Distrust of all mankind, and readiness to strike the first blow for the safety of his own life, have therefore become the maxims of the Afridi. If you can overcome this mistrust, and be kind in words to him, he will repay you by great devotion, and will put up with any punishment you like to give him except abuse.'

The Afridi of the Khyber have changed little over the years. Even today the traveller entering the Pass has the sense that he is entering a unique world of violence and honour that has somehow stood aside from time. Barely fifteen kilometres from Peshawar, the bazaar at Jamrud, which marks the southern entrance to the Pass, throngs with tribesmen. They have strong, chiselled features and piercing eyes which vary in shade from black through burning amber to green. To anyone coming here for the first time from the lowlands of Pakistan, perhaps the strangest thing about them is that they are all armed, usually with rifles, ranging from old British Lee Enfields to modern Russian Kalashnikovs, but sometimes with automatic pistols or sub-machine-guns. As you wander amongst them outside Jamrud's tea-shops and provision stores, you will feel them meeting your curiosity with theirs. They are ready to be friendly, to talk and to exchange news, but you have the sense that these are people with whom liberties cannot be taken. Everything about them seems to signal 'thus far and no further'. They handle their guns with an easy familiarity and show them off with a half-serious, half-mocking bravado that suggests that murder may not be far away. It is not, and never has been. Lives on the frontier today are still taken with the same disdainful ease as they were a century ago when the British tried to make safe the road through Khyber to Kabul and Kipling wrote:

Above: Saffron-rice breakfast for a group of Afridi tribesmen in the bazaar at Jamrud. The town stands at the entrance to the Khyber Pass, and is a melting pot where frontier people gather to share the rich border trade with Afghanistan.

A scrimmage in a Border Station—
A canter down some dark defile—
Two thousand pounds of education
Drops to a ten rupee jezail—
The Crammer's boast, the Squadron's pride,
Shot like a rabbit in a ride.

The British left behind a number of mementos of their long stay in the Khyber. The road itself is the most enduring, while the weathered and faded insignia and crests of famous regiments carved into the glowering slate walls of the Pass are the most evocative. There is a railway too, dating back to the mid-1920s. The sight of the steam train which, once a week on Fridays, runs up from Peshawar to Landi Kotal, reinforces the sense that one has of the Khyber Pass being outside the normal processes of time.

The train has an engine at either end—both were made in England in 1931. Clouds of steam belch forth as it chugs up and down the gradients of the Pass and in and out of the tunnels. As it pulls into the shelter of the massive red-brick walls of Shagai Fort, built in the centre of the Khyber at around the same time as the railway, a passenger could be forgiven for thinking that the price of his ticket had taken him not on a journey from place to place but on a journey back into another era.

A stiff climb above Shagai stands an empty picket-fort that commands a sniper's-eye view. The wind blows through its rifle slits and machine-gun turrets and whips under the sill of its heavily-armoured iron door, sadly recalling battles of long ago and the lonely soldiers far from home who fought them.

The British first arrived on the frontier in 1849, but did not get any real control of the Passes until the Second Afghan War, which was fought between 1878 and 1880. Though there was a curious kind of mutual respect between the British and the tribesmen, real peace was never established in the region. History records that more than forty British military expeditions were obliged to take the field between 1858 and 1902 and that, in 1897, 40,000 troops were required to quell the Afridis.

By the turn of the century Afghanistan had become a buffer-state between the British Empire in the subcontinent and the Russian Empire in Central Asia. The British were by then well-established in the Khyber, which had taken on an important rôle in the playing-out of the global strategy described by Kipling as 'the great game'. The primary British concern was to keep the road open. This is what their quarrels with the Afridis were mainly about. Winston Churchill wrote that the tribesmen regarded the whole tendency towards road-making 'with profound distaste'. All 'people were expected to keep quiet, not to shoot one another, and, above all, not to shoot at travellers along the road. It was too much to ask ...'

The British never did manage to govern successfully the hills above the Passes, where endless small-scale battles were fought right up to the partition of India and the independence of Pakistan in 1947. One British officer wrote of a campaign in the late 1930s, 'We felt as if we were using a crowbar to swat wasps.' Even today, central government has not fully extended its control over the tribal belt, a fact that is clearly evident to anyone driving through the Khyber Pass. Here, in the heart of their territory, the Afridis are still very much a law unto themselves. Each extended family lives within a high-walled enclosure, more like a medieval fortress than anything else, built from mud, stones and timber. Armed sentries patrol outside the makeshift corrugated iron gates to protect property and women from the prying eyes and greedy intentions of hostile neighbours. The larger structures seem to have been designed to withstand long sieges with their own gun-turrets, and with the minarets of family mosques rising above the walls.

The Afridis are Sunni Muslims. They take their religion seriously, interpreting the dictates of Islam in the strictest and most orthodox manner. But even in this aspect of their lives they find room for a fierce self-parodying humour. According to a probably apocryphal tale that tribesmen still delight in telling, a holy man came to the Khyber Pass many years ago from the south: 'He preached to our fathers of their sins and upbraided them. He pointed out that in all our country we did not have a single tomb of a saint at which we might make our devotions... Our fathers were much impressed with this holy man's words. So they killed him, and ever since his tomb has been a noble shrine.'

The Afridi are a division of the Pathans, the most numerous tribal people in the world, and surely one of the most remarkable. As the last British Governor of the Frontier, Sir Olaf Caroe, has written in his

authoritative book *The Pathans*, 'The persistence of the Pathan tribal tradition has produced a society at all levels, starting from the nomad and the herdsman, through the articulated tribe and the sponsors of an Asian dynastic principle, to the modern lawyer, engineer, doctor, administrator and politician. Standing over against the tribal village and the tents of the caravan are men for a century imbued with Western thought and now reaching forward to that synthesis of values which Pakistan strives to attain. All these stages of development can be seen today, side by side and superimposed one on another, by anyone who cares to move in a twenty-mile radius around Peshawar. By so doing it is possible to enjoy daily a bodily translation into earlier phases of human society and life ... We have here ... a congeries of peoples engaged in a long march through the centuries from the fifth to the twentieth.'

Who are the Pathans and what is it about the society they have forged that gives it the special quality of being able to blend the ancient with the modern, while at the same time retaining an essential cultural integrity? Other tribal societies all over the world have shattered like brittle glass under the impact of the twentieth century; individuals have become alienated and schizophrenic; once-sacred customs have been touted on the streets before tourists for a few pennies. So why have the Pathans remained unaffected?

Part of the explanation, anthropologists say, lies in the nature of the environment inhabited by the Pathans; for those who wish to maintain and cherish their traditions, what better place to do it than in the rocky defiles and rugged hillsides of the frontier? As Caroe observes, 'The authority of the various empires which claimed in the past to rule this frontier really only extended to control over the plains and one or two passages through the mountains. Only the greater Mughals seem to have thought it worth their while to make a serious attempt to bring the hill-tribes under domination as subjects, and they failed. Even passage by a main route through the mountains had often to be asserted by force and with difficulty against the refractory tribes which held the road in use at the time. An understanding of this fact explains the escape of this tribal belt as a whole from subjugation to any external power—a freedom symbolized by the failure to impose upon it any taxation. This, too, is the reason why a tribal form of society has persisted in a country which lay across the passage of countless invaders...'

Left: The fortress-like houses of the Afridi tribe in the Khyber reflect the character and outlook of the people who built them. The larger structures have been designed to withstand long sieges and house several families.

There is more to the endurance of the Pathans than just environment, however. These are a people who have built up a social system that is resilient in its institutions and governed by a granite-hard ethical code. The essence of this code is honour. 'I despise the man who does not guide his life by honour,' wrote the great Pathan poet Khushal Khan Khattak, 'the very word "honour" drives me mad.'

The code of the Pathans is called *Pukhtunwali*, and although it is nowhere written down or formalized, every Pathan knows what is required of him.

First and foremost, he must be ready to revenge any insult or any harm done to him, to his family or his clan. This obligation is called *badal* and is nicely summed up in a local proverb: 'He is not a Pathan who does not give a blow for a pinch.'

The workings of *badal* have led to innumerable feuds up and down the frontier, most of which originate because of disputes over *zar, zan* or *zamin*—gold, women or land. If, for example, Gul Khan feels that his wife has not been shown proper respect by Ali Khan he may respond by slapping Ali Khan. Seeking his own revenge for this blow, Ali Khan may produce his knife and stab Gul Khan in the arm. Gul Khan could then legitimately respond by drawing his revolver and shooting Ali Khan dead. The next thing that will happen is that one of Ali Khan's relatives will lie in wait for Gul Khan and eventually kill him, as the *badal* principle requires. A relative of Gul Khan's will then be obliged to kill a member of Ali Khan's family, and so on. Affairs like this can last for several generations, have been known to wipe out whole families, and can even be transported overseas. More and more Pathans these days are leaving Pakistan as migrant workers, so one need look no further than the concept of *badal* to explain the apparently unmotivated killing of one Pathan by another in far-off Dubai or Jeddah, for example. The point to remember is that Pathan custom, unlike Western law, is much more concerned with the satisfaction of the aggrieved than with the punishment of the aggressor.

The second pillar of *Pukhtunwali* is *melmastia*, hospitality to guests. Any traveller through Pakistan's tribal belt, once invited in by a Pathan, will be given a generous welcome and quickly made to feel at home. Even the richest and proudest *Malik*, or traditional elder, will personally serve tea and biscuits, or sometimes a full-scale meal to his guests, whatever their social status. Every *Malik* has his own guest-house where visitors are offered rest, food and shelter, and each Pathan village will also have at least one communal guest-house, and possibly two or three, to enable it to extend hospitality to travellers. Another

Above: Afridi tribesman rests his rifle at a tea-stall in Jamrud Bazaar as he drinks green tea. The favourite beverage of the Pathans, it is served with style and ceremony.

facet of *melmastia*, which it has always been much harder for Westerners to fathom, is the right of sanctuary whereby the true Pathan is required to afford protection to anyone who asks it of him, even common criminals fleeing the law.

The main institution of Pathan society, and the only institution for the arbitration of honour feuds, is the *jirga*, an assembly of tribal elders called to decide specific local issues. *Jirgas* may have as few as five members or as many as sixty. Only exceptionally, if for example a dispute between two major tribes is involved, will a larger *jirga* be called.

James Spain, a diplomat and writer, has described the *jirga* as 'the closest thing to Athenian democracy that has existed since the original.' *Jirga* decisions are taken by consensus rather than by a majority and the *jirga* does not normally determine guilt or inflict punishment, but rather aims to achieve a settlement that will satisfy all parties. Other duties are to make decisions concerning community property, for example the location of a mosque, and to convey the wishes of the clan to other clans and also to outsiders.

The *jirga* has few sanctions at its disposal to enforce its will. Nevertheless, to all intents and purposes, the word of the *jirga* is the only *law* the Pathans have or are prepared to accept. Travelling through the frontier areas one is first struck and even alarmed by this apparent *lawlessness*, but a closer acquaintance with the Pathans reveals an order and a structure to their affairs. They are true anarchists in the sense that they will bow to the authority of no central government; however, they know what to expect of one another and that, today as in the past, seems to be enough.

The total Pathan population is estimated at between fifteen and seventeen million, of whom about nine or ten million live in Pakistan and the remainder in Afghanistan. Their physical features vary from place to place but they all speak one or the other of the two dialects of *Pashtu*, a language belonging to the Indo-European family. They use neither racial nor linguistic characteristics to identify themselves as a distinct and separate people: they say that a Pathan can be recognized by his adherence to *Pukhtunwali*; if he acts in accordance with the code then he is a Pathan and if he does not, then he is not a Pathan.

Pathans have shown a remarkable ability to adapt to urban life, although they are essentially a people of the countryside and of the mountains. Peshawar, only a few kilometres from the Khyber, is, in its own way, as much an expression of Pathan society as the smallest village high up in a remote hill pass.

The name Peshawar means 'frontier town' and the modern city still has about it a wild and woolly pioneering look, although it combines this with a centuries-old streetwise craftiness. Most of the goods brought to market in Peshawar today come in on the back of gaudily-decorated trucks. However, camel-caravans, or *kafilas*, are still a common-enough sight in the spring, led by hard and sturdy men from the surrounding hills eagerly anticipating the rough-and-tumble bargaining of the bazaars. Once again the visitor has the sense of time not passing quite as it ought to. Kipling's 'Ballad of the King's Jest', written in the nineteenth century, is as true today as it was then:

When spring-time flushes the desert grass,
Our kafilas wind through the Khyber Pass.
Lean are the camels but fat the frails,
Light are the purses but heavy the bales,
As the snowbound trade of the North comes down
To the market square of Peshawar town.

The best-known part of Peshawar is the Qissa Khawani Bazaar, the Street of the Story-Tellers. In the old days, before radio and television provided a quicker medium, it was a place where news and views were exchanged and where professional raconteurs enthralled large audiences of passers-by.

A walk down Qissa Khawani today is still an exciting experience. Although the story-tellers are long gone the street still throbs with activity. Colourful fruit-stalls and sweet-shops compete for your attention with wayside restaurants selling a bewildering variety of kebabs, grilled meats and freshly-baked unleavened bread. The aromas of tea and cardamom seed fill the air and mingle with sandalwood, incense and tobacco in a heady cocktail. Vendors proclaiming the virtues of their wares switch languages with ease as one customer moves away to be replaced by another. Pashtu, Farsi, Urdu, Punjabi and English all seem to be spoken with equal fluency.

The bustling sidewalks and the road itself—where motor cars, horse-drawn cabs, and pedestrians jostle for right of way—confirm the cosmopolitan nature of the crowd. An American tourist in blue jeans and sandals haggles over the price of a bag of oranges. A wandering fakir, from the plains of India, heavily bearded and dressed in foul-smelling rags, stands belligerently in the middle of the road swinging a huge wooden club at the passing traffic. A group of Afridi youths, fresh from the Khyber and ready for anything, walk four-abreast through the

Opposite: In the Qissa Khawani Bazaar, Peshawar's famous Street of the Story-Tellers, a pony-trap competes with pedestrians for right of way.

crowds. A smokey-eyed Mahsud from the far south of Pathan territory pauses to sip green tea, glancing warily over the rim of the small china cup as he does so. Two women, covered from head to foot in thick white pencil-pleated *burkas*, that make them look like giant shuttle-cocks, flit up a side alley leaving behind just the faintest impression of dark and beautiful eyes behind the veils, of jewelled ankles and small delicate feet painted with henna beneath the clumsy garments.

At the end of Qissa Khawani, near the heart of Peshawar's Old Town, the street takes a sharp turn left into the Bazaar of the Coppersmiths. Here finely-worked plates and samovars, teapots and vases, glitter in narrow recessed stalls in the doorways of which the craftsmen sit cross-legged on comfortable cushions talking to each other or fashioning copper with light blows from a small hammer. The smiths are proud

Opposite: Peshawar Bazaar craftsman 'Poor Honest Ali' panels rich and intricate detail on his traditional hand-beaten copperware. His superb work has been presented to several heads of state, including Queen Elizabeth II of Great Britain.

and skilled men, and several of them have achieved international acclaim. One of the most popular is Ali, who somehow manages to make a major ceremony out of every sale, no matter how small. First he brings out a selection of his best wares from the back of his stall. Then, after a purchase has been made, he offers tea and shows the customer his photograph album, in which he features with at least half a dozen heads of state. 'I am only a poor man,' he says, 'but even a poor man can sell his work to great leaders if his work is good enough.' Ali signs his ornate pink business cards P.H.Ali. The P and the H, he says, stand for Poor and Honest. 'I am Poor Honest Ali. Not Ali the Lion of God; not Ali Baba and the Forty Thieves; not Prince Ali Khan; not Mohamed Ali Clay—just Poor Honest Ali.'

From the Bazaar of the Coppersmiths it is only a few minutes walk to the central square of Old Peshawar, Chowk Yad Gar. The square is a traditional site for political rallies and for meetings of all kinds. Off it is the Bazaar of the Goldsmiths and the Silversmiths, a narrow, steeply-rising street with high old buildings on either side that cast the whole area into a perpetual dusk. In this hot half-darkness the jewellers display bangles and necklaces, rings and pendants, behind glass cases. The atmosphere of intrigue is increased by the money-changers who have installed themselves in the same street and who sit, crouched protectively over colourful piles of paper currency, doing their mathematics on pocket calculators.

The Bazaar of the Goldsmiths and the Silversmiths forms the approach to the Mahabat Khan Mosque, built by Peshawar's Governor in the 1670s during the rule of the Mughal Emperor Aurangzeb. As you enter the mosque from the busy, narrow street, a restful silence envelops you and the bustle and barter of the commercial world is left behind. Here people come to pray or to rest themselves during the heat of the afternoon by the cool fresh pool in the tiled centre of the wide square courtyard. No one is turned away. Rich and poor alike may pause here to contemplate beneath the soaring white minarets and the open and breathless sky.

Peshawar was already old when the Mahabat Khan Mosque was built. Its streets had long been divided out amongst the specialized and distinct trades and professions that still monopolize them today: silversmiths and coppersmiths, physicians and dentists, pharmacists and cobblers, carpet-weavers and cloth merchants, bird-sellers and rice huskers, to name but a few. Century after century of trade and commerce at the crossroads of Asia and the subcontinent have given the smokey alley-ways and teeming bazaars of the Old Town a unique character.

Peshawar's origins go back at least 2,500 years and probably much further. Herodotus wrote about the city in the fifth century BC, calling it Kaspaturos. By the second century AD it had become the capital of a thriving Buddhist empire that once extended over much of Pakistan, India and central Asia.

Though nothing of Buddhist culture remains in Pakistan today, the frontier area was considered by pilgrims 2,000 years ago to be the second home of Buddhism. The subcontinent's first true emperor, Chandragupta Maurya, a contemporary of Alexander the Great, laid the political foundations for the spread of Buddhism. It is his grandson, Asoka, however, whom historians credit with implanting the religion throughout the north-west which, at that time, about 250 BC, was known as Gandhara.

Following the death of Asoka in 235 BC, the Mauryan Empire collapsed and was replaced by a series of city-kingdoms ruled, in turn, by Bactrians, Indo-Greeks, Scythians and Parthians. Buddhism in Gandhara survived and prospered despite the political turmoil, and entered its golden age around AD 64, when the stable Kushan dynasty was founded by invaders from the north.

Gandhara culture had always been strongly urban-based, and became even more so under the Kushans, who were good businessmen and did much to promote trade. It was during this period, at the end of the first century AD, that Peshawar first rose to prominence, superseding Charsadda as the capital of Gandhara. It even outshone Taxila, which was a major centre of learning at that time and the site for Asoka's massive Dharmarajika ('Royal Law') stupa. Today, while Peshawar still thrives and expands, both ancient Taxila and Charsadda are in ruins. The broken-down walls and dilapidated monuments of Taxila are sprawled out over a large, grassy site about twenty-four kilometres from Islamabad and eighty from Peshawar. Thirty-two kilometres north-east of Peshawar, all that is left of Charsadda, once dubbed Pushkalavati, or 'Lotus City', is a dusty and overgrown mound of earth seventy feet (twenty-one metres) high.

Peshawar became rich under the Kushans and made the best of its position at the entrance to the Khyber Pass on the silk route to China. All that remains in the modern city to remind us of the flowering of Buddhist culture, art and architecture, however, is an interesting museum. Tradition says that the Buddha himself walked the streets of Peshawar long before the Kushans, and predicted that a great king would be converted there, who would build a stupa which would be burnt down and rebuilt seven times. History says that the Kushan king Kanishka was converted to Buddhism in Peshawar around AD 128 after watching a young street-boy making a model of a stupa out of cow dung. Kanishka later built a stupa on the spot which was 620 feet (189 metres) high and was topped off by twenty-five gilded discs on a tall mast. The stupa was burnt several times in the sixth and seventh centuries, after being struck by lightning. Today it is a mound of stone and rubble only a metre or so high in the centre of the huge Shah-ji-ki-dheri cemetery which stands about one and a half kilometres to the south-east of Peshawar.

After the demise of the Kushan Empire in 241 Gandhara gradually began to decline as a centre of Buddhist culture. The region was invaded from the north by the White Huns in the fifth century and many of the monasteries were looted and razed to the ground. The monks were forced out of the cities and sought sanctuary in the hills and valleys, where they managed to hold out in isolated pockets for several hundred years. However, the golden age was over. Hinduism enjoyed a brief resurgence in the region during the ninth and tenth centuries but gave way to Islam at the beginning of the eleventh century when Mahmud of Ghazni swept down out of Afghanistan and captured Peshawar.

Peshawar has been an Islamic city ever since, achieving great eminence under the Mughals during the sixteenth and seventeenth centuries. The massive walls of the Balahisar Fort were originally built by Babur just before his death in 1530, then extended by the Sikhs during their brief and unhappy rule here in the early nineteenth century. The Sikhs, who showed scant respect for the religion of the Peshawaris, were faced with a series of rebellions and revolts which they are reported to have quelled by hanging four citizens from the beautiful minarets of the Mahabat Khan Mosque each week.

In 1849 the British came to Peshawar and built a cantonment to house their officials and troops. Though the British have gone the cantonment lingers on, giving off the faint, nostalgic aroma of Empire. The nostalgia is strongest at Dean's Hotel which, like Raffles in Singapore and the Norfolk in Nairobi, belongs to the era of Somerset Maugham, of gin slings and tiffin, and of The White Man's Burden. The hotel consists of a series of chalet-bedrooms tightly grouped around a central dining-hall where meat and two veg, or curries for the more adventurous, are served in traditional Imperial style.

The broad tree-lined avenues of the cantonment, the neatly-laid-out parks, and the bungalows set amongst brightly-flowering gardens, contrast sharply with the narrow streets and vivid crowded bazaars of the Old Town. Peshawar offers yet more contrasts, however, with its graceful University campus centred on Islamia College, now more than sixty years old, and with the ultra-modern educational and research institutions, including a nuclear-medicine centre, which have sprung up since Independence. Many years ago Lowell Thomas called Peshawar 'the Paris of the Pathans'. The traveller passing through the city today will agree that the description is still a valid one.

Overleaf: Peaceful view of the Kohat Valley, which has achieved notoriety for its gun-making industry. The valley is better known on the frontier simply as the Darra—a generic Pashtu word meaning 'pass'. The town of Darra Adamkhel at the heart of the valley is the centre of the frontier's booming gun trade.

The road south out of Peshawar leads to the remarkable village of Darra Adamkhel. There Pathans can be seen indulging in their favourite activity—buying and trying out guns ranging in size from tiny lethal toys shaped like pens which fire a .22 bullet, to massive automatic anti-aircraft weapons and howitzers. Darra is only a little more than forty kilometres from Peshawar but the contrast that it presents to the leafy gardens and dreamy Academe of Islamia College could not be more complete.

Indeed, there is nothing academic at all about Darra Adamkhel. It is a very down-to-earth, business-like place. It trades in death as it has done for more than a hundred years. It is the main centre in the region for indigenous arms manufacture and its craftsmen boast that, in addition to their own designs, they can copy any gun made by man. Darra is famous for its excellent replicas of the British Lee Enfield .303 rifle, and dozens of these are still produced each month. Webley .455 revolvers and Sten guns are other traditional stalwarts. Since the 1970s the gunsmiths of Darra Adamkhel have also been experimenting with more modern technology and now churn out copies of the Russian Kalashnikov automatic rifle and of the Pakistan Army's own G3. A few of the workshops specialize in heavier weapons and, on receipt of firm orders from a customer, will produce howitzers and even anti-aircraft guns.

Opposite: Life in the little town of Darra Adamkhel revolves around the manufacture of guns and ammunition. With surprisingly little modern machinery the gunsmiths of Darra make accurate copies of all sorts of guns, including automatic weapons like the Russian AK47, howitzers, and big-bore anti-aircraft guns. The old British Lee Enfield .303, however, is still the most popular amongst the tribesmen of the frontier. Prices vary from about 140 rupees for a cunningly-designed pen gun to 10,000 rupees for a good copy of a Kalashnikov and 15,000 rupees for a .303. Top left: Drilling the muzzle of a .303 carbine. Bottom left: Filling shell cases with explosive powder. Far right: Customers in a Darra gun shop.

Opposite top: Malik Shere Khan of Darra Adamkhel. Much decision-making is done by tribal elders known as Maliks, who wield considerable power. Malik Shere Khan owns most of the property in Darra Adamkhel and is widely respected both for his wealth and his wisdom.

Opposite bottom: Demoiselle Cranes are pet birds of Malik Shere Khan. They are, he proudly tells visitors, 'better than watchdogs' in warning of intruders.

Guns made in Darra are priced not only on the amount of craftsmanship that has been involved in their manufacture, but also on the size and killing-power of the individual weapon. Pen guns are sold for as little as 140 rupees, revolvers start at 400 rupees and automatic pistols at 800 rupees. Sten guns retail at anything between 1,000 and 2,000 rupees and heavier machine-guns at 7,000 rupees upwards. Cheap small-bore rifles can be had for as little as 500 rupees; but a really good copy of the aristocratic Lee Enfield can cost as much as 15,000 rupees. Kalashnikov replicas, called *Dangar* in Pashtu, (the word means animal) generally take one man about a month to make and are sold for about 10,000 rupees.

Customers are welcome to try out guns before purchasing them, provided they are prepared to pay for the amunition which, in the case of the Kalashnikov, costs about 7 rupees a round. A customer can only claim a refund or replacement for a defective gun if he returns it before sunset of the same day.

Apart from the fact that its inhabitants do not wear ten-gallon hats, and tend to ride camels instead of horses, Darra Adamkhel is straight out of the Wild West. It consists of a single, long main street on both sides of which are ranged the gaudily-decorated gun-shops, occasionally interspersed with tea-stalls and general stores. Everywhere turbanned men dressed in sandals and the baggy trousers of the frontier are to be seen gazing lovingly at the murderous displays. One may be loading up a pistol, another sighting down the barrel of a .303 at an imaginary enemy, a third lets off long bursts from a Kalashnikov into a nearby hillside, while a fourth discharges the entire magazine of a tommy-gun into the air. It takes some time to get used to the sound of gunshots and to repress the instinct to dive for cover.

Back from the street, behind the shops, in a warren of narrow muddy alley-ways and low-roofed buildings, are the 'factories' in which all of Darra's guns are made. Some individual craftsmen specialize in rifle-barrels or in firing mechanisms, others make only cartridges, repetitively filling the brass casings with highly explosive powder and then tapping home the bullets with indifference. In a number of the bigger workshops a complete production line exists with raw metal and wood at one end emerging at the other as beautifully-fashioned rifles or machine-guns.

According to Malik Sher Khan, the senior elder of Darra Adamkhel, and the town's richest man, 'A gun is a pre-requisite for security of life. In order to survive you have to possess a gun.' The Malik argues that, despite the profusion of weapons, the town is peaceful. 'Of course there are some accidents, but we have very few killings here and there are no *dacoits*. No one wants to kill anyone else or steal from anyone else because they know that they will be hunted down and killed in their turn if they do. This is because every man has the means to defend himself. It creates a kind of balance. If some men did not have guns and others did then the balance would be lost.'

The word *darra* means 'valley', or 'pass', in Pashtu. The Adamkhel are Afridis, and the suffix *khel* means 'group of' or clan: so the town is named after and belongs to the Adam group of the Afridi tribe of the Pathans. The *darra* itself, more commonly known as the Kohat Pass by foreigners, connects Peshawar to the town of Kohat, and marks the southern extreme of Afridi territory.

Opposite and right: Brightly decorated coaches and lorries ply up and down the frontier taking people from village to village in a never-ending round of movement and commerce. The most ornate vehicles get the most passengers.

*Above: On the road from Bannu to Peshawar,
Khattak farmers separate the wheat from the chaff
in much the same way as their forefathers have
done for centuries. The crop is first crushed and
then forkloads of it are thrown into the air. A light
breeze carries away the chaff in a yellow haze and
the wheat falls to the ground.*

South and east of Kohat, and around Bannu, the traveller enters the land of the Khattaks. A story about their origins illustrates the Pathan sense of humour: Pathan women have always gone about heavily veiled, probably since pre-Islamic times. The story is that Lukman, the progenitor of the Khattak tribe, was out hunting one day with three of his brothers when they came across four young ladies wearing *burkas*. One of the brothers proposed that lots should be cast for the women and that they should then marry them. Lukman, however, would have nothing to do with this scheme, insisting that since he was the eldest he should choose his bride-to-be. Lukman selected the one who was best dressed and his brothers cast lots for the other three. When the time came for unveiling it was discovered that Lukman's choice was very plain, dark and stout, while the other women were beautiful. The younger brothers began to laugh and jeer saying, '*Lukman pah khatey lar*' which, roughly translated, means 'Lukman has dropped himself in the mud.' Ever after he was known by the nickname Khattak—'stick in the mud'—and this name was given to his descendants also.

The Khattaks are famous for their dance, variations of which are also popular with other Pathan tribes up and down the frontier. In its unadulterated form the dance is a hypnotic spectacle as up to twenty men, armed with long glittering sabres, swirl and turn to the deep barking rhythm of a drum. The turns and cuts that they execute begin slowly and ponderously but build up into a complicated frenzy of blurred movements. The dancers' eyes become glazed and vacant and they seem to be participants in a wild martial ritual, entranced and indifferent to life or death.

To the west of Khattak country is the beautiful Kurrum Valley, which runs from Kohat to Parachinar on the border with Afghanistan. The road follows the winding course of the Kurrum River along the valley floor, which is green and fertile, producing crops that vary from wheat and rice to spinach and opium. Here the people belong mainly to the Turi tribe and, although they speak Pashtu and follow the *Pukhtunwali* code, they are different from other Pathans in a number of ways. The most important by far of these differences is that many of them are Shia Muslims rather than Sunni. However, the traveller who journeys through their fields and villages will notice more their gentleness, chivalry and fine manners, which contrast sharply with the rough-house attitudes of the tribes that surround them. This gentleness is perhaps a reflection of the environment in which they live, which is blessed with a fine Alpine climate.

Above: The Khattak dance, performed to the barking rhythm of a drum, is hypnotic. Up to twenty tribesmen swirl and turn with sabres in their hands as though preparing for war. The dance is traditional to the Khattak clan of Pathans but has been adopted and developed by other frontier tribes.

Overleaf: Seen from the Kurrum River, the white-tipped mountains of the Safed Koh Range stretch across the horizon in a breath-taking panorama beyond rice paddy fields. This is a prosperous farming area which also produces crops of wheat and maize and is famous for its fruit orchards.

At the head of the Kurrum Valley, nestling amongst apple orchards and tall plane trees called *chinars*, is the Turis' regional capital Parachinar. On its sloping, unpaved streets, fruits and vegetables of all kinds are sold and the people live a simple, uncluttered and spiritually pure life, rarely out of sight of the single tall and graceful minaret of the town's mosque. The twentieth century is still regarded as an interesting and possibly dangerous novelty by most of the inhabitants of the region who, quite rightly, take what they want from the modern world and leave the rest to others. Thus Parachinar lacks night-clubs and hotels but does have several first-rate schools. When the weather is good, as it is almost every day in the summer, classes are held out of doors so that rural parents, many of whom are still not at all sure that education is a good thing, can come and see for themselves what it is all about. 'Slowly and gradually,' a teacher explains, 'old traditions and customs are giving way to the new light.'

Parachinar is ringed by a number of smaller villages whose very names, Shalozan, Ziaran Qubadshekel, summon up an image of Shangri-La. Here, in the foothills of the 16,000 foot (4,877 metres) high 'White Mountain', so-called because its summit is never free from snow, farmers practise an intense form of cultivation, using terraces and complicated irrigation channels to get the best out of every scrap of available land. Even in high summer there is a healthy chill in the air and the people wear brown or grey rough-spun woollen caps called *bakol* which are indigenous to the region and which, when winter comes, can be rolled down to protect the ears and neck from frostbite. Delicate, elfin-faced children dart in and out of the farmhouses, pausing to stare with unselfconscious curiosity at the occasional stranger who intrudes upon their world.

Just to stand in the midst of this countryside in the hour after dawn can be an uplifting experience for those with the eyes to see, the ears to hear, and the openness of spirit to accept the natural beauty of simplicity. While the menfolk tend sheep and cattle in the remoter pastures, dark-robed women work the home fields, their high, gentle voices mingling with the chuckle of the swift icy streams running down from the mountains. Far away a cock crows and a dog barks, the sounds carrying crisp and clear across the intervening kilometres. The early morning sun thrusts a relentless warmth through the sharp Alpine air as the shadows of night lift from the fields of wheat, rice and artemesia.

Opposite: Parachinar mosque, with the perpetual snows of the 16,000 foot (4,877 metres) 'White Mountain' in the background. Parachinar, with its clear invigorating air, green meadows and apple orchards set against high mountains, seems like a Swiss Alpine village.

Westwards from Parachinar, only a few kilometres over the mountains, is the border with Afghanistan. Southwards and eastwards, on the road that follows the course of the Kurrum River, is the town of Thal, where the Turis gradually give way to the Daur tribe and then to the Wazirs and the Mahsuds in the wilds of Waziristan.

From Thal onwards, travel is inadvisable without an armed escort. James Spain, the American diplomat who journeyed through much of the frontier in the 1950s and early 1960s, explains why: 'Here *Pukhtunwali* is the only way of life. Here the Pathan may be found at his cruellest—and his noblest. Here great and proud men have tasted defeat and humiliation. . . . The very landmarks have grown out of dark and bloody deeds: the tree under which a British political agent of long ago was murdered by his trusted orderly because the orderly took insult from his master's gift to a fellow tribesman of a rifle better than his own; the curtain-shrouded bedroom where another political agent shot himself because the government refused to honour his promises to the tribes; the Shahur Tangi, a narrow defile between Tank and Wana, where a British convoy was cut to pieces in an ambush in 1937.'

The road between Thal and Miranshah, the regional capital of North Waziristan, runs through a sterile, windblown desert that contrasts bleakly with the green terraces and fertile rolling hillsides of Parachinar. Here the Wazirs have fashioned castles from sand and stone. Walls confront walls, all the gates are closed, and all the windows have been narrowed to rifle slits. If ever a place were to be chosen to illustrate the theme that man is an island unto himself, this would be it. The rough battlements set back from the road proclaim a universal suspicion and an all-encompassing mistrust.

Miranshah commands the Tochi Pass through the Waziristan Hills on the Afghanistan border. Here, within a well-fortified cantonment, a succession of Political Agents have tried to mediate between central government and the intractable tribes. Between 1910 and 1912, the first man to do this extremely difficult job, which calls for rare qualities of tact, diplomacy, cunning and charm, was Major-General C. A. Smith. The current Political Agent for North Waziristan sits in the same cool, roomy office that Major-General Smith occupied, beneath a varnished but fading wooden honours-board on which are inscribed the names of all his forty predecessors. The tasks of the Political Agent have hardly changed at all since the turn of the century. The *jirgas* of the Wazir tribe

Above: Young girl carrying water near the town of Parachinar, North-West Frontier Province. The people of Parachinar have a shy and gentle manner.

Right: In the still of early morning, women return to the village of Ziaran Qubadshekel with crops from their vegetable gardens. Pathan women cover their faces unless sure no strangers are about.

Opposite: Pathan children enjoy the early morning sun on the flat roof of their house in the village of Miaran Qubadshekel. The houses in the village are constructed of stone and mud strengthened with wooden beams—a design capable of absorbing the shock of the region's frequent earthquakes.

are still summoned to the office to explain and resolve kidnappings or murders on the main highway, and other serious matters where the concerns of the government and the actions of the tribesmen come into conflict. Here, too, unsummoned, the *jirgas* come to discuss tribal grievances with the Political Agent and, if possible, to win concessions from him. Once, after spending more than two hours in closed session with forty hawk-faced, bearded *Maliks*, and plying them, in the traditional fashion, with sweet English tea and small ginger biscuits, the Political Agent emerged to describe the members of the *jirga* as 'very clever negotiators', adding, 'They know what they want and they won't be fobbed off with delaying tactics. You have to have your wits about you all the time or they'll get the better of you.'

Sir Olaf Caroe tells an amusing story of an earlier *jirga* in Miranshah: 'The *jirga's* spokesman was a grey-beard named Shahzar, a man of great presence but with a twinkle in his eye. The *jirga* wanted something done; the presiding officer, as is often wise, gave a diplomatic answer which put off the evil day. Said Shahzar: "Sahib, you remind me of a story I heard at my mother's knee. There was once upon a time a King, and of course the King had a Wazir, and seeing that the Kingdom was beside a river like our valley, there was also a fisherman in the realm. One day the fisherman caught—uff!—an enormous fish and, as in duty bound, presented the catch to the King. But the Wazir, like all Wazirs, who expect perquisites, thought ill of this. The fish should have been presented through him and he was annoyed. So thinking to get the fisherman into trouble, he said to the King: 'Your Majesty, enquire of this fisherman if this fish is a male or a female.' So the King laughed and said to the fisherman: 'O fisherman, say, is this fish a male or a female?' But the fisherman saw the trap; whatever he said, male or female, he would be ordered to go and catch its mate, and this he would never be able to do as it was the finest fish in the river, and he could never catch another worthy of it. So he replied: 'Your Majesty, this fish is a hermaphrodite.' And Sahib," concluded Shahzar, "your answer reminds me of that fish."'

Overleaf: Camel-train loaded with timber on its way to market in Miranshah after an eight-day journey from the Afghan hills.

Miranshah, as well as being the seat of the Political Agent, is a major market-place. Its bazaar burgeons with colourful mulberries and small, yellow, peach-like *logarts*. Its streets, like the streets of any frontier town, are full of armed men. Swarthy dark-turbanned Wazirs and Mahsuds intermingle in an atmosphere of controlled aggression. Of the two tribes, Caroe wrote, 'It is not so hard to distinguish one from the other, not by his dress, for that is much the same, but by something indefinable in his air and carriage. The nearest I can get to it is to liken the Mahsud to a wolf, the Wazir to a panther. Both are splendid creatures; the panther is slyer, sleeker and has more grace, the wolf-pack is more purposeful, more united and more dangerous.'

Opposite: Baskets of freshly-picked mulberries and logarts in Miranshah bazaar. The town is an important market for frontier trade.

Miranshah's main industry is raw timber brought down from the forest in the surrounding hills, eight days' journey away, and sold at a substantial profit to the local building industry. The timber market stands outside the main town and, like so much else in the Pathan lands, outside time as well. Were it not for the distant vapour trail of a jet aircraft in the powder-blue sky above the Afghan mountains, you could imagine yourself transported back to the days of Genghis Khan as the camel-caravans file in out of the desert. From a kilometre or two away, against the shimmering heat-haze of morning, a long *kafila* has a dreamlike quality, as the big burden-camels pick their way slowly forward on huge, two-toed splayed feet. The features of the men who walk alongside gradually become more distinct as they approach, and the visitor can see the lean, tough, lawless look that they have, accentuated by the array of weapons they carry and by their clothes, which are dirty and sweat-stained from the long march. Each camel is laden with four huge, rough-hewn logs, and as they finally enter the market they need little persuasion from their masters to collapse on to their knees. Ropes are then pulled and the logs tumble down with a dull thud on to the dry earth while the camels grumble their appreciation. 'The bubbling camels beside the load,' Kipling wrote a century ago, 'sprawled for a furlong adown the road.'

As the day wears on the logs are collected and stacked into piles three metres high, and the merchants come in their lorries and pick-ups to make their purchases. The bargaining is fierce and noisy and extends far into the night. As darkness falls fires are built and meat is roasted and the whole area takes on the mediaeval atmosphere of a giant nomadic camp, preparing for war perhaps, or festivities, in a mood of expectancy: 'And there fled on the wings of the gathering dusk, a savour of camels, of carpets and musk, a murmer of voices, a reek of smoke . . .'

South of Miranshah the traveller enters a land populated virtually exclusively by Mahsuds, described by one turn-of-the-century writer as 'the most independent, intractable and turbulent tribe on the frontier'. Even today passage through this country to the main towns of South Waziristan, Tank and Wana, is not recommended. Dera Ismail Khan, a little further to the south on the left bank of the Indus, can be reached more easily from the Punjab by crossing the river.

East of Miranshah, after the town of Bannu, the road back to Peshawar passes once more through Khattak country. Here the people still farm the land in much the same way as their forefathers have done for centuries. The wheat is still separated from the chaff, as it has been since Old Testament times, by first crushing the crop and then throwing forkloads of it into the air. A light breeze carries away the chaff in a yellow haze and the wheat falls back to the ground. Here, too, the

Opposite and above: Gypsies on the long march from the Indus Valley to the highlands of Afghanistan. They spend summer in the mountains returning to the plains when winter comes. Gypsies are called Powindas *in Pakistan, a word that means simply 'nomad'. Most are Pathans and all speak Pashtu. More liberal in their customs than other Pathans, women walk unveiled in public.*

traveller may see ancient water-wheels still in use. Occasionally goaded by shouts from small children, a blinkered ox or cow tramps round in a never-ending circle, turning a gear that dips a rope of earthenware pots into a fresh-water well forty feet (twelve metres) deep. As the pots rise to the surface they tilt over, spilling their contents into a metal conduit that leads to an irrigation channel.

The road continues northwards through Kohat and Darra Adamkhel and eventually leads back to Peshawar. From there a number of routes lead out of the wild country of the Pathans. Of all of these the one that most repays the journey passes through the remote and lovely Swat Valley which was, until 1969, an autonomous princely state under a Pathan leader of the Yusufzai tribe, known as the Wali of Swat.

Entry to the Swat Valley is through the high Malakand Pass that separates the town of Mardan to the south from Saidu Sharif to the north. It was in the Malakand, around 1515, that the invading Yusufzais surprised a Swati garrison and forced their way through to Saidu Sharif. More than 350 years later Winston Churchill, who had enlisted with the Malakand Field Force, saw action in the Pass against the Yusufzais in the great uprising of 1897.

The road through the Malakand winds along the valley side in a series of steep hairpin bends and precipitous curves. In places it is not wide enough to allow two vehicles to negotiate it at the same time. The Yusufzai bus and truck drivers, however, who are apparently indifferent to death, do not regard this as an obstacle and maintain consistently high speeds, avoiding collisions with obvious reluctance by braking ferociously at the last minute. As the vehicle in which you are travelling skids to the road's unguarded edge in a cloud of dust, and you look down in horror at the 1,000 foot (305 metres) drop to the valley floor below, you can at least console yourself with the poignant beauty of the view.

The Pathan poet Khushal Khan Khattak said of Swat that it was 'meant to give kings gladness'. It gives gladness to ordinary people too. At its widest point, where the Swat River runs relatively slowly through a series of meanders, the countryside is open and fertile and blossoms with wild flowers and rich crops. The kaleidoscope of colours from trees, bushes and fields, the rarified invigorating air, the blue skies scudding with far-off clouds, the hot midday sun reflecting off the rippling waters of the river, the warmth and hospitality of the people; for all these reasons, Swat is rightly described as a paradise.

Certainly, the Buddhists found it so when they fled here from the wrath of the White Huns in the fifth and sixth centuries. They called Swat *Udyana*, or 'garden', and, because of the valley's remoteness behind the natural barrier of the Malakand, Buddhism survived here far longer than it did elsewhere in Pakistan, not giving way to Islam until the eleventh century.

Opposite: The Swat Valley, once a centre of Buddhist culture in Pakistan, has many ancient relics including the 1,500-year-old seated Buddha carved into a cliff face above the town of Jehanabad. Although visible from the main road, the 20 foot (7 metres) high carving can only be approached on foot after an hour's walk. The track passes an ancient unexcavated stupa.

Below: The Butkara ruins outside the town of Saidu Sharif at the foot of the Swat Valley are the site of an ancient Buddhist temple. The carved figures depict a scene from the life of Buddha. The lion, which is in ancient Greek style, was carved by a craftsman from a nomadic Ionian tribe.

Below: The famous statue of the 'Fasting Buddha' at Lahore Museum. Almost 2,000 years old, it is a reminder of the Gandhara period in north-western Pakistan, when Buddhism was the dominant religion.

As a result, many reminders of the Buddhist era remain. The most substantial of these is to be found just over a kilometre from the well-endowed Swat Museum in Saidu Sharif. Called Butkara, the recently-excavated site has produced a large selection of carvings, statues, jewellery and decorated columns. Though the passing of the centuries has reduced most of the original structures to rubble, the outline of the massive central stupa is still clear, as are the remains of the more than 200 smaller stupas that ringed it.

Further up the valley, a few hundred metres from the main road, is the Shingerdar Stupa, which is still reasonably well-preserved. Its origins are not known for certain, although some scholars identify it with a stupa mentioned by the Chinese pilgrim Hiuen Sang who visited this region in the seventh century. Hiuen said that the stupa was built by Uttarasena, an ancient king of Swat, as a shrine for some relics of Buddha that he had in his possession.

By far the most beautiful and imposing monument that the Buddhists left behind in Swat is a carving of the seated Buddha in the sheer rock on a hillside above the village of Jehanabad, about sixteen kilometres north of Saidu Sharif. According to Buddhist lore, the Buddha himself came to Swat in his last incarnation as the Gautama Buddha, and preached many sermons telling the people of the lessons that he had learned in earlier lives. After he had completed a particularly moving sermon a stone stupa emerged miraculously from the place where he had stood. It is on this 'stupa'—a pile of boulders—that the Jehanabad Buddha is carved. His view looks into the setting sun over a peaceful valley and green terraced hillsides. In the tranquillity of early evening the poetry and grace of the carved figure and its calm untroubled gaze speak of a state of mind that mankind in the twentieth century seems to have lost forever.

Saidu Sharif, the traditional seat of the Wali of Swat before the one-time princely state was fully absorbed into modern Pakistan, makes an excellent centre from which to explore the lower Swat Valley. The splendid Swat Hotel, two storeys of large, spacious rooms arranged in a square round an attractive garden bordered with flowers, is worth visiting in its own right. It was built by the Wali when the increasing number of visitors to Swat could no longer be accommodated in the official guest-house of the palace after the Second World War.

The Pathans of Swat, like their cousins further south, are farmers and traders. Around Saidu Sharif, however, a good deal of river fishing, both licensed and unlicensed, is also done. One of the sights of the lower valley in the early morning is village children up to their waists in water, patiently trawling for their breakfasts with hand-nets. Here, too,

Opposite: Precarious 30-year-old raft, a jaala, *looks like the forerunner of the modern inflatable dinghy and consists of four inflated cow skins. The* jaala, *an ideal form of river transport in the Swat Valley, being light-weight and portable, is carried upstream and then launched to drift downstream with goods and passengers.*

a unique kind of boat can occasionally be seen. Called the *jaala*, it consists of a light wooden frame supported on inflated cow hides. Looking from a distance like giant water bugs, these boats skim across the surface of the river carrying people and merchandise from one side to the other. They are propelled by a pair of rough oars in the brawny hands of the steersman, and a reasonable degree of control can be maintained even in fairly rough water. The *jaala* is confined to the lower Swat, however; further up the river runs too quickly for even the sturdiest craft.

Overleaf: The confluence of the Unkar and Utrot rivers at the head of the Swat Valley. The waters of the Utrot are coloured brown with sediment from the valley floor, while the Unkar, a mountain torrent, is still crystal clear.

The road up the Swat Valley from Saidu Sharif passes through dramatically changing countryside as the foothills of the great Himalayan range give way to true mountains and high snow-capped peaks. At Bahrain the river has become a rushing torrent of muddy grey water and the valley has narrowed to a few hundred metres. A tributary joins the Swat here and the confluence of the two waters creates a subdued roar of sound that echoes perennially amongst the curious high buildings of the little town. Bahrain marks the northernmost limit of the Pathans of Swat. Hereafter the valley is inhabited by Kohistanis—'people of the mountains'—who are of mixed racial origins and who speak many different languages.

At the head of the valley is the village of Kalaam where the wild Ushu and Utrot rivers sweep in out of the pine forests in a great fork to give birth to the Swat. The Pakistan Tourism Development Corporation hopes to develop Kalaam as a holiday centre and has built a chalet-style motel there. Certainly the scenery rivals anything that the Swiss Alps have to offer as the rising sun flushes the snow-capped peaks of the surrounding mountains a soft flamingo pink. However it is to be hoped that the people of the Ushu and Utrot valleys above Kalaam will not have their age-old privacy spoiled by unsympathetic tourists.

The proof that tourism is not always a blessing is brought home in the valleys of Birr, Bumburet and Rambur, two days' hard trek over the mountains to the north-west of Kalaam. The 3,000 people who live in these valleys are known as Kalash. They are the only community in Pakistan that has not adopted Islam, and their unique pagan religion and unusual culture have made them a focus of interest to travellers the world over. In the last ten years they have been literally swamped by curious tourists, who fly in from Peshawar or from Islamabad across the 16,000 foot (4,877 metres) Lowari Pass to the town of Chitral. From Chitral, jeep treks are organized into the Kalash valleys thirty-two kilometres away and the tribespeople are paid to stage their dances, which were originally meant as heartfelt celebrations of the changing seasons, whenever enough tourists appear.

There is something deeply disturbing and pathetic about the way in which the Kalash culture is being diluted and degraded by its head-on collision with the cash economy of the twentieth century. It is a comment on the world in which we live that a people who have stood back from the consequences of countless invasions, and adhered to their traditions for centuries despite the huge changes being wrought around them, should today at last give way before the combined onslaught of the aeroplane and the four-wheel-drive vehicle.

Opposite: *Quizzical Kalash girl expresses her doubts about the presence of strangers. Kalash society is gradually being weakened and diluted by the effects of tourism; nevertheless, the traditional charm and innocence of these people remain unspoilt.*

Though it is true to say that Kalash culture in its original form no longer exists, due to the exposure that it has received, the Kalash are still a fascinating group and there is much about them that repays genuine study as opposed to the casual and uncommitted attention of the tourist.

The Kalash live in about twenty small but long-established villages scattered through the three valleys. Their houses are compact, generally windowless, structures made from alternate layers of timber and stone, or timber and unbaked brick—a design that architects recognize as being to some extent earthquake-proof. As a rule the

Above: Traditional Kalash dance performed to celebrate the arrival of spring. The dance is slow and rhythmic, characterized by the steady beat of the drum and by the high-pitched chant of the dancers.
Right: Kalash peasant farmers mix cultivation with goat-herding.

Smiling young Kalash girls of northern Pakistan, last survivors of a pagan culture which once claimed a million followers. Today, however, the Kalash number only a few thousand confined to three isolated valleys in the Chitral region. Many have light skin and sandy-coloured hair. Some researchers believe they are descended from the armies of Alexander the Great which passed this way in the fourth century BC. The curious cowrie-shell head-dresses of the women certainly suggest these people moved to this remote part of the subcontinent from somewhere nearer the sea. The Kalash, however, have no written language or recorded history to prove this theory.

villages are set amongst trees and sited close to rivers. If you ignore for a while the continual pestering requests of the children for money—or, even better, pay them off—and stand still amongst the quiet well-shaded houses in earshot of running water, then it is still possible to pick up the faint echoes of the reverence for nature that was once so central to Kalash life.

Kalash religion has been described as 'a unique form of polytheistic paganism with distinctive elements of animal sacrifice and of nature and ancestor worship'. According to Lieutenant-Colonel Afzal Khan, who lived in Chitral for several years and studied the Kalash closely, 'they believe in a number of gods, goddesses, saints, fairies and demons. But there are two particular divinities who enjoy special veneration— Mahandeo and Jestak. Mahandeo has a marked character as a virile warrior-god who protects the crops, birds and hunting. He is, in fact, protector of the Kalash village and Kalash territory as a whole. Jestak, on the other hand, has a feminine personality. She is the protector of the home and the private life—pregnancy, birth, children, love, marriage, etc.'

Kalash means 'black' and refers to the black clothing worn by the inhabitants of Birr, Bumburet and Rambur. Kalash women, dressed in their black robes, simple bead jewellery, and cowrie-shell head-dresses, make an unusual and imposing sight. Many of them are fair-haired and green- or blue-eyed, reinforcing the theory put forward by a number of anthropologists that the Kalash may be descended from the army of Alexander the Great. The Kalash language, *Kalashwar*, seems to contain elements of Greek, Persian and Sanskrit, which also indicates that the Kalash community may be a mixture of Indo-Aryan and Greek races.

The Chitral district, in which the Kalash valleys are situated, is an area of great natural beauty. The town of Chitral itself, in sight of the towering peak of the 25,290 foot (7,708 metres) Tirich Mir, and situated along a curve of the Mastuj River, is an invigorating and pleasant place to visit. Here is the fortress and palace of the Mehtar of Chitral, the traditional ruler, largely unoccupied now but still with its faded mementos of times gone by. In 1895 a British garrison was besieged in Chitral Fort for a period of six weeks during an uprising.

The relief force that broke the Chitral siege on 18 April 1895 was led by Colonel Kelley and had marched across country from the town of Gilgit, roughly 350 kilometres to the east. The journey then took nearly a month but would not take so long today. The Pakistan Army's Frontier Works Organization, which has its headquarters at Gilgit, is busy constructing a new network of all-weather roads throughout the northern areas. These roads have cut down journey times significantly and have opened up the entire region to development and to travellers.

Gilgit is situated in country over which are strewn some of the world's highest mountains—the Karakoram Range—and across which pour some of the longest glaciers outside the polar regions. Here, since time immemorial, people have grouped together into scattered and separate valley communities with distinct identities and life-styles. Behind the natural barriers of the environment tiny kingdoms have risen and fallen unnoticed, and mediaeval wars have been fought out to themes of chivalry and treachery long forgotten by the outside world.

Within a 160-kilometre radius of Gilgit there are a hundred peaks of over 18,000 feet (5,486 metres) including K2 which, at 28,250 feet (8,610 metres) is the world's second-highest mountain. The town of Gilgit is dominated by the 25,550 foot (7,788 metres) Rakaposhi while Nanga Parbat, 26,660 feet (8,125 metres) high, towers over nearby Juglot.

These huge, perennially snow-clad peaks give birth to glaciers, rivers of hard-packed ice sometimes more than sixty-four kilometres long, including the Batura in the upper Hunza Valley, the Hispar and the Biafo, the Pasu and the Baltoro. The mountains are also run through with a chain of small lakes, which, from above, look like emerald and turquoise gem-stones. By far the most beautiful of these lakes is Kuchura, which is located to the south-east of Gilgit near the town of Skardu. Rama Lake in the Astore Valley rivals Kuchura in scenic charm, but its higher altitude means that it is frozen over for much of the year.

Gilgit itself stands on a narrow, fertile plain entirely ringed around by mountains, and enjoys a generally pleasant climate except for about two months in the summer when it becomes oppressively hot. Its people are for the most part farmers, tending fruit orchards in which apricots are the main crop, although apples and pears are also plentiful.

Gilgit has a long history and, as the eighth century Buddha carved thirty feet (nine metres) up on a rock face in the Kargah Nullah six and a half kilometres outside the town proclaims, it has seen several empires rise and fall. In the more recent past, from 1842 to 1847, Gilgit was occupied by the Sikhs. Later the British took it over and for a while, at the turn of the century, it enjoyed great importance in their strategy to oppose Russian expansion.

Opposite: Precarious houses on ledges carved out of the treacherous scree slopes of a mountain near Chitral are linked by a fragile web of precipitous footpaths. In this region good agricultural land is scarce and even the steepest hillsides are terraced and planted to produce crops.

Following pages: Baltoro Glacier, 58 kilometres long, covered with rocks split by frost from mountainsides through the centuries, forms the main approach to the high Karakoram Range.

Pasu Glacier flows down the Pasu Peak in the main axis of the Hunza Karakoram Range, at points overhanging the Karakoram Highway connecting Pakistan with Tibet.

The Deosai Plains, ice-covered, wild and lonely are a high-altitude plateau in the Karakoram above Skardu. They are marked by the desolate beauty of Lake Shersar (foreground), which is frozen for most of the year.

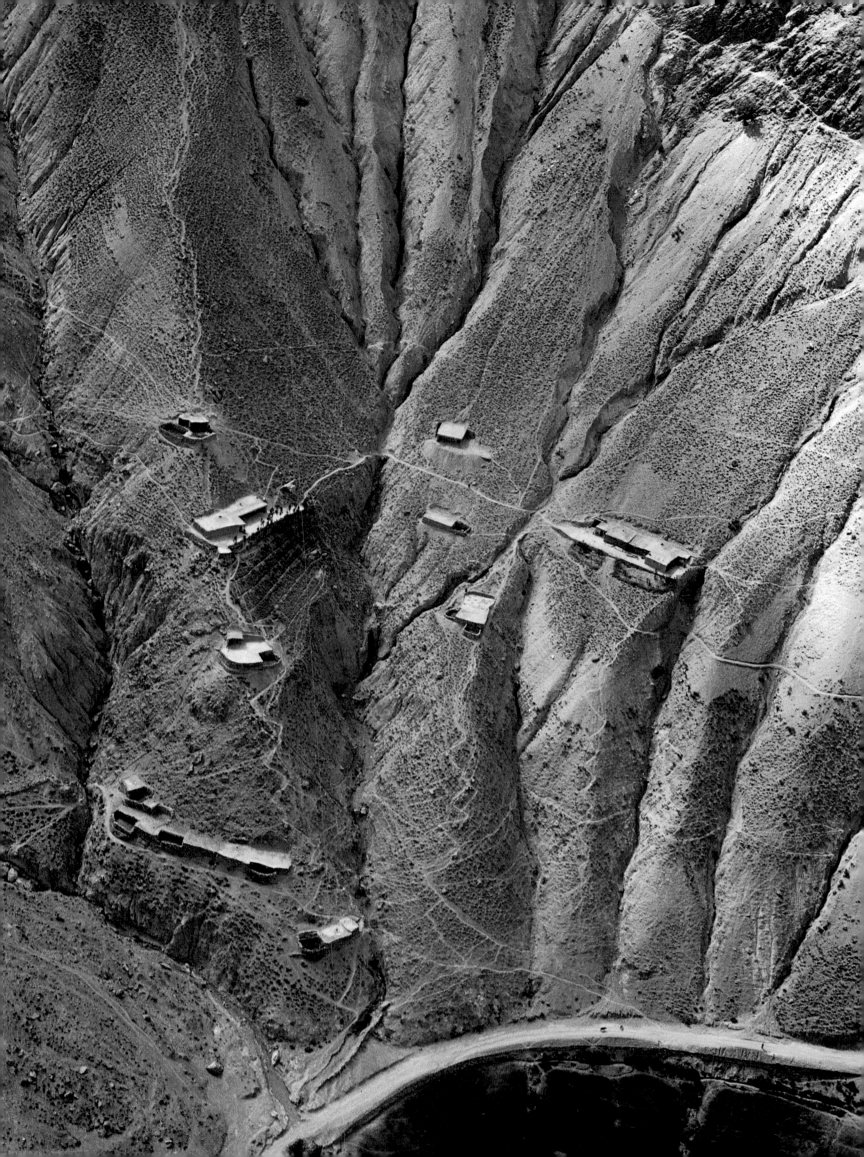

During their stay in Gilgit the British learned to play polo, a game indigenous to these northern areas. The game is still popular with the Gilgitis; indeed it is almost an obsession. During the tournaments, which are held regularly, all work stops and the entire town turns out to watch. Throughout the region every village has its own polo field and sometimes as many as thirty teams gather together at Gilgit to compete.

Right: Venerable Mohamed Hussain, who claims to be 101, still does an honest day's work every day of the week. A Balti from Sordas village, about 32 kilometres from the town of Skardu, his attitude to life is philosophical: 'When God takes me,' he says, 'I will go.'

Leaning low from his saddle, a player thunders forward in an attacking move during a polo tournament in Gilgit (left). Tournaments start with competitions aimed at testing each player's prowess with the cavalry lance. Wooden tent pegs or cylinders of paper are stuck upright in the ground as targets (below). The use of lances suggests the martial origins of the game of polo, which was born centuries ago in the Gilgit area. In Gilgit polo has no maximum or minimum number of players, although seven-a-side is preferred. Rough and exuberant, the rules are loosely applied. Any tactics may be used to score a goal, including hand-carrying the ball over the line. Generally the game is conducted in good spirits but sometimes, (opposite) emotion overcomes an opponent.

When a big tournament is on, Gilgit assumes a carnival atmosphere
and horses and men decked out in colourful regalia parade up and
down the main streets. There is much pomp, circumstance and pride
and each player seems by his bearing to proclaim agreement with the
words carved on the gates of the polo ground: 'Let other people play at
other things; the king of games is still the game of kings.'

Before the tournament begins there is a display of tent-pegging in
which the players arm themselves with long lances and, at full gallop,
attempt to spear short cylinders of rolled-up newspaper stuck into the
ground. Co-ordination, stamina, fine judgement and a good aim are
called for to hit the target and these are much the same qualities that go

Circumcision of a male child in Gilgit, an occasion of great rejoicing marked by music and festivities. Opposite: Guests take turns to dance and watchers place money in their caps. The amount each dancer earns reflects his status in the family but, by tradition, the money goes to the musicians. Right: Dressed in elegant finery, Zaid, Mohamed and Ali, aged seven, five and four, Muslims of the Shia sect, await their circumcision.

Overleaf: Yasin Valley, at the foot of the Hindu Kush range in northern Pakistan. Barely a century ago the inhabitants of Yasin lived in a constant state of war with their neighbours from Gilgit and Hunza. The Valley today is peaceful and prosperous, its patchwork of fertile fields producing a variety of cereal and fruit crops.

to make a good polo-player. Perhaps the most important quality of all, however, is enthusiasm—plus a certain amount of aggression. When the game finally starts the players throw themselves into it with surprising violence and vigour, and there is much clashing of sticks and forceful horsemanship. Throughout the match musicians in the sidelines playing pipes and drums keep up a heavy skirling rhythm which increases in pace and rises in pitch whenever a player charges towards goal.

Gilgit on tournament day is a cosmopolitan place, acting like a magnet to the brightest and the best from all the surrounding valleys. A number of different tribes speaking several different languages—Shina

Above: Ismaili children working in the fields near Sultanabad, a little town to the north of Gilgit. The Ismaili sect has many adherents in this part of Pakistan and the Aga Khan, their spiritual leader, is a popular and revered figure.

and Boorishki are the main ones—are to be found in the region and, although all are Muslims, several different sects are represented, including Shia, Sunni and Ismaili.

The Ismailis, whose spiritual leader is the Aga Khan, are concentrated in the Hunza Valley, which was once a tiny self-contained state ruled over by a king known as the Mir. The opinions of those who see Hunza tend to vary with the season in which they see it. At the onset of winter it gets very little favourable comment. John Keay, author of *When Men and Mountains Meet*, had this to say of it: 'There are no pools for fishermen, no falls for the photographer, and no grassy banks for the picnicker, just this thundering discharge of mud and rock. . . . It is a revolting sight, less a valley or gorge than some gigantic quarry.' By contrast, Eric Shipton, who must have visited Hunza in the spring or summer, described the valley as 'the ultimate manifestation of mountain grandeur—the most spectacular country I have ever seen.'

At its best when it is bedecked with flowers, and with its fields flush with ripening crops, Hunza looks like a fairyland. This impression is strengthened by the turrets of the 650-year-old Baltit Castle, the traditional seat of the Mir which, high on a hillside, overlooks the valley. The men, going leisurely about their daily tasks, are small and wiry with fine ruddy features. The women, partially veiled, wear colourful baggy trousers, knee-length shirts, and embroidered flat-topped caps. Hunza houses are small, rude structures of undressed stone with low doorways, and are generally grouped together in 'families' of a dozen or more surrounded by an outer wall. This kind of defensive architecture was dictated by the state of war which existed for several hundred years between Hunza and its counterpart mini-kingdom of Nagar, on the other side of the valley.

Beyond Hunza's capital Karimabad, there are no further settlements of any size in Pakistan. The country rises steeply and becomes increasingly bleak and chilly, scarred by half-frozen streams and laid over with patches of ice and frost. In this wilderness, perhaps because so few men come here, rare Marco Polo sheep, with their huge curving horns, still survive—though in declining numbers. Snow-leopards, too, are sometimes sighted here. Herds of wild yak forage in the hard earth.

Above: Tall evergreens provide shade in Karimabad, capital of Hunza Valley, with the new Palace of the Mir of Hunza (foreground), home of the traditional ruler of the valley. Hunza is at its best when bedecked with flowers and flush with ripening crops.

Opposite: Hunza houses are small, crude structures of undressed stone with low doorways, grouped together and surrounded by an outer wall. This kind of defensive architecture was dictated by the state of war which existed for several hundred years between Hunza and its counterpart mini-kingdom, Nagar, on the other side of the valley.

Right: The elf-like features of a young Hunzakut child enhance the fairy-tale atmosphere of the Hunza Valley.

Overleaf: Highest tar road in the world, the Karakoram Highway has opened up Pakistan's northern areas, improving trade and communications with the south and bringing isolated villages closer. It was built by Pakistan's Frontier Works Organization and cuts across tough country, winding and turning through icy mountain passes.

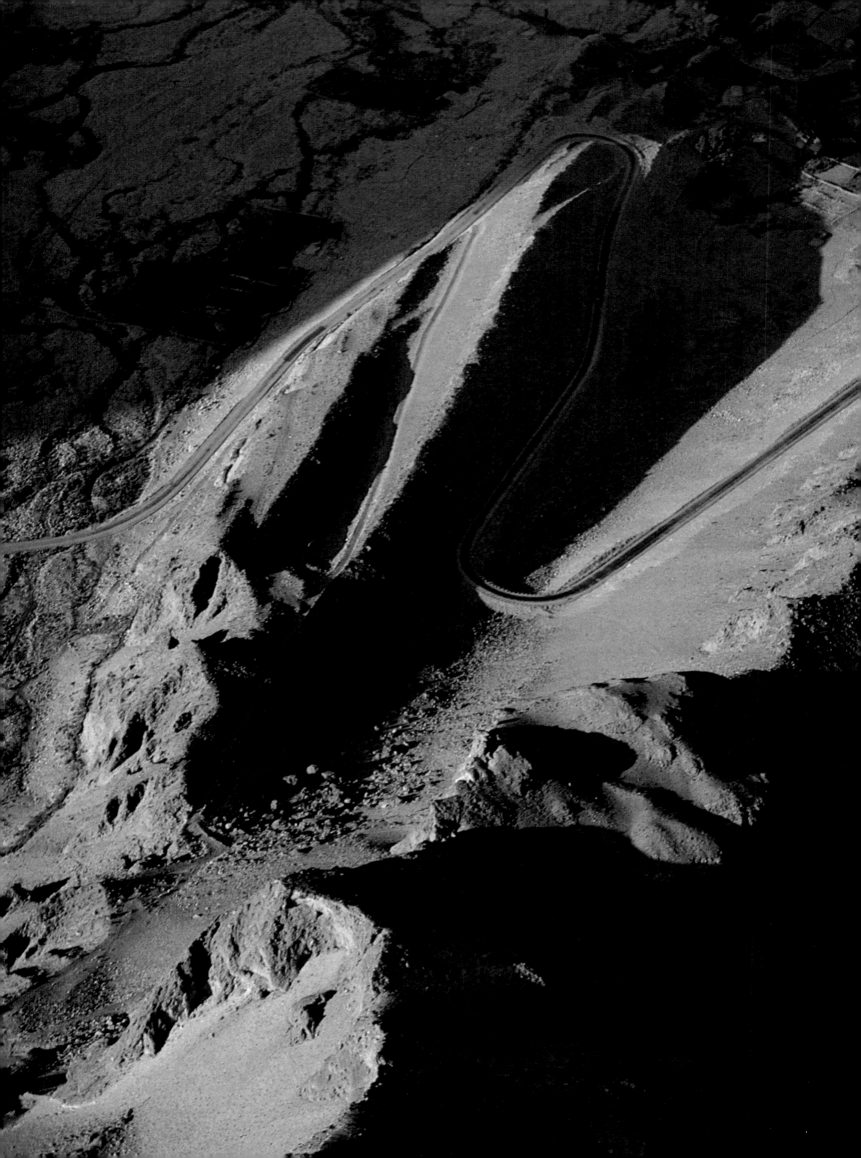

At the top of the Khunjerab Pass, at an altitude of 15,072 feet (4,593 metres), is the border with China, unmarked by any customs post. The air is so thin that even the slightest effort is exhausting and one wonders how it was possible for men to build a road here. Yet a road was built and is now recognized as one of the wonders of the modern world. Standing on Khunjerab Top the great Karakoram Highway seems to go on and on ahead of you forever, into the limitless distances of China. Behind you it winds back through the valleys and along the side of the Indus River as far as Thakot, 616 kilometres away, where it joins up with Pakistan's main-road network.

The Karakoram Highway (KKH) was a co-operative venture between

Right: Khunjerab Pass on the border between China and Pakistan where the great Karakoram Highway straddles the roof of the world and the air is so thin that the slightest physical effort is exhausting.

China and Pakistan, and was largely built by the Pakistan Army's Frontier Works Organization. One life was lost for every kilometre of its length. Experts say it will take fifty years for the rock structures on which much of the road is grounded to settle properly, so it is certain that, in the continuous task of maintenance that lies ahead, many more engineers and labourers will die. No one who has worked on the road or been associated with it in any way, however, begrudges this human cost. Not only is the KKH taken as a symbol of national endeavour and pride but, in a very real sense, it has helped to unify the nation by bringing the previously remote northern areas within a day and a half's journey of the capital city.

The drive down the Karakoram Highway is an experience that is unique in the world. The road winds and turns in icy mountain passes, crosses and recrosses the Indus on Bailey Bridges, soars along the side of the valley hundreds of metres above the thundering waters and cuts repeatedly through sheer rock. The journey from Khunjerab to Thakot, like no other journey in Pakistan, impresses upon the traveller the vastness and variety of this country and the endeavour and resilience of its people. In the passing of a day the frontier lands, with all their raw magic, have been left far behind. Ahead of you the road points like an arrow to Islamabad.

Opposite: Treacherous scree covers precipitous slopes tumbling down to a mountain stream in the Astore Valley. Subject to frequent landslides and earthquakes, the valley sides are scarred by the precarious courses of old roads swept away and then rebuilt on new alignments.

Overleaf: Murree, one of Pakistan's most popular hill-resorts, enjoys a warm, invigorating climate in the summer and ski-able snow during winter.

Chapter Three The River and the Plains

Islamabad, Pakistan's federal capital, is a new city standing back-to-back with an old one—Rawalpindi. The two street-plans hint at very separate identities. Islamabad is divided into functional squares and rectangles; Rawalpindi (better known simply as 'Pindi') sprawls across the map with all the accidental irregularity of ancient human settlement. A drive through the cities confirms this first impression. Islamabad's quiet suburban charm, its atmosphere of hushed officialdom, and its green, tree-lined avenues, contrast sharply with Pindi's vigorous commercialism, its noisy bustling markets and its dusty streets thronged with traffic. Nevertheless, the old and the new are intimately connected. The planners saw Islamabad and Pindi together eventually expanding into a massive twin-city with a population of up to six million sharing common urban services and amenities. Though a megalopolis on this scale is still a long way off, there is no doubt that Islamabad-Pindi is already a reality for the citizens of the two communities. There is a high degree of social and business contact and traffic moves constantly on the dual-carriageway that joins the city centres.

The idea for Islamabad emerged some years after the independence of Pakistan. It became apparent that Karachi, though in every way the commercial capital of the country, had many shortcomings as an administrative centre for federal government. In 1959, therefore, a commission was appointed to select a location for an entirely new city, and eventually the present site was chosen, on the recommendation of Doxiades Associates, urban-planners for Athens. A master plan was then drawn up for Islamabad, setting off the urban area against the backdrop of the Margalla Hills to the north and Rawal Lake to the south. Construction work started in October 1961, directed by many world-famous architects and planners including Ponti and Edward Durrell Stone. By 1964 Islamabad's first residents—mostly federal civil servants—had started to arrive. Today the city is a fully functional federal capital with a population in excess of 175,000.

Travellers entering Islamabad for the first time are struck by its greenness. More than six million trees have been planted here since the foundations were laid. The result is that, from the air, the capital seems to have been thrown down in the midst of virgin forest. Most of the buildings are low, rarely exceeding two storeys, and this makes it difficult to get a perspective on the city from anywhere within its boundaries. The best viewpoint by far is the Daman-e-Koh, a terraced garden on the Margalla Hills from where it is possible to see the whole of Islamabad spread out before you, dominated by the towering minarets of the new Shah Faisal Congregational Mosque, and by the Houses of Parliament. A light haze seems to lie over this city ringed around with mountains and caught between the green earth and the powder-blue sky. The air, at some 1,700 feet (518 metres) above sea-level, is fresh and bracing. The nights are cool throughout the year and there are even occasional light snowfalls in winter.

Above: Panoramic view of Islamabad. Work on Pakistan's federal capital started in October 1961 and it has become a busy, sophisticated city. The main urban area is laid out against the backdrop of the Margalla Hills in the north and Rawal Lake in the south. More than six million trees give the city a green and pleasant look.

A closer acquaintance with Islamabad reveals the careful planning that has been put into it as it has expanded and grown. The gentle, undulating land on which the city lies has been made a feature of a spacious and aesthetically attractive layout divided by function into eight distinct zones—administrative, diplomatic, industrial, commercial, and so on. The residential areas are laid out as a series of self-contained townships which reflect the traditional character of the neighbourhood in Pakistani towns and have their own shopping and recreational centres, educational and health facilities. Because of this 'cellular' design Islamabad has largely managed to avoid the soullessness so common in other new towns and cities throughout the world; nevertheless, it will be many years before it shrugs off its 'show-case' atmosphere and becomes completely settled in its ways, with its own character.

Fourteen and a half kilometres to the south, Rawalpindi presents a sharp and total contrast to Islamabad's brave new world. Not far away, in the Soan Valley, some of the earliest Stone Age relics in the subcontinent have been found, dating back about half a million years. They belong to an era when the climate and the landscape differed significantly from the present day and when the Himalayan snow mantle spread downwards towards the plains. Modern Rawalpindi dates back to around the fourteenth century when it was destroyed and subsequently rebuilt by the Mughals. Later, in the nineteenth century, the British arrived and turned it into a major cantonment town garrisoned by many thousands of troops, whose responsibility it was to guard the North-West Frontier. The cantonment atmosphere persists today, as does its associated military flavour, for Pindi is the General Headquarters of the Pakistan Army. Most notably, however, this is a town of transients, a pleasant place in which to stop for a night or a week on the road through Murree to Kashmir for travellers from the west or south.

Pindi stands square on the ancient Grand Trunk Road, 162 kilometres from Peshawar and 275 kilometres from Lahore. Because it is at such a significant crossroads the town's bazaars— Saddar, Raja, Sarafa and Murree Road—offer an absorbing pot-pourri of the produce and workmanship of the neighbouring regions: Kashmiri silver, shawls and jackets; Bokhara carpets; embroidered *kurtas* and woollen kaftans; cane baskets, furniture and walking-sticks. All these things, reminiscent of other places and peoples, beckon the traveller outwards and onwards.

Women of Pakistan. Black and white trouser and smock combination (opposite) contrasts with attractive red and white striped Shalwar Qamiz in teeming Rawalpindi. Hands held pensively, an attractive young Pakistani girl (left) gazes dreamily into the future. Young son at her arm (above), a Rawalpindi mother shops in busy bazaar area. Centuries of traditional modesty are symbolized in the discreet black veil of an urban housewife (above left).

*Above: Sheepskin hats and coats in Murree bazaar,
a hill-resort which is often covered with several
inches of snow in winter.*

A two-hour drive to the north of Pindi, at an altitude of more than 7,500 feet (2,286 metres), is the picturesque hill-resort of Murree and the Gallies. Here during the coldest months of the year there are deep and lasting snowfalls making possible a variety of winter sports. The time to visit Murree, however, is in the spring, when the pine-scented hillsides blossom in a multitude of colours. The word *galli* signifies a valley between mountains and there are many of these in the Murree area. Probably the best-known settlement is Nathiagalli which stands beneath sheltering forested slopes at an altitude of 8,000 feet (2,438 metres), roughly midway between Murree and the town of Abbotabad.

Northwards again from Abbotabad lies the gently beautiful and peaceful Kaghan Valley, 153 kilometres long and ringed around by the mountains of the Himalayas and by lakes, waterfalls and glaciers. Near the head of the valley, guarded by forbidding peaks, is Lake Saif-ul-Muluk, some 10,500 feet (3,200 metres) above sea-level. Here a prince of long ago is rumoured to have fallen in love with Badri Jamal, a fairy princess.

The territory immediately south of Rawalpindi offers different but equally worthwhile scenery, as the Potwar Plateau, on which both Pindi and Islamabad are built, gives way to rich and fertile lowlands. These territories, lying directly on the pathway of many of the invasions to which the subcontinent has been subject throughout its history, were occupied by the Persians from the fifth to the fourth century BC and then, briefly, by the Greeks under Alexander the Great. Towards the end of the sixth century AD the White Huns invaded the Punjab, ushering in a long period of instability that was only brought to an end in the eighth century with the arrival, from the south, of the Muslims who set up a forward base at the town of Multan. Some 800 years later, the establishment of Mughal rule by the Emperor Babur saw the beginning of a golden period in the Punjab's history that is still remembered in the folk-tales of the people with both warmth and respect.

Below: Brightly painted pottery makes an eye-topping splash of colour on a Taxila street. The bustling modern town with its handicrafts is in sharp contrast to the silent slumber of the 2,000-year-old ruins of the ancient city nearby which was once a centre of learning and of Buddhist culture.

Below: Well-known Taxila potter, Abdul Rashid, at work outside his shop painting the tall jars unique to the area.

Rhotas Fort, a dramatic reminder of the Mughal period, is to be found near Jhelum, some 109 kilometres to the south of Rawalpindi. This famous stronghold was built in the 1540s by Sher Shah Suri and served as a headquarters for his campaigns against the militant Gakkhar tribes of the Punjab. The fort, subsequently extended and developed by Akbar, is one of the most impressive historical monuments in Pakistan and dominates the surrounding countryside. The massive, towering walls, in some places more than forty feet (twelve metres) thick, enclose an area of 260 acres. Although they are now somewhat dilapidated it is still possible to make out the ruins of the sixty-eight towers and twelve gateways which once adorned them.

Southwards from Jhelum, the road runs on kilometre after kilometre into the seemingly endless agricultural plains of central Pakistan, covered with thick green carpets of cotton, sugar-cane or wheat. The obvious wealth of the region is a reflection of the energy of its peoples rather than of any special environmental benevolence, for the land is essentially desert despite the five rivers that run through it and give it its name. *Punjab* means 'five waters' and these are the Beas, the Jhelum, the Chenab, the Ravi and the Sutlej rivers. In the distant past cultivation was confined to the river banks and to small areas near artesian wells. About one thousand years ago, however, ambitious farmers began to construct canals. By the time of the Mughals, the canal-system had become lengthy and complex and provided a basis for real prosperity. Later the British added to the network, making it the most extensive in the world.

Irrigation on this scale has, today, made the Punjab the most productive and economically active region of Pakistan, supporting a population of more than forty million. By far the most visible symbol of the economic activity, and of the fact that the people have money in their pockets, is the colossal amount of traffic borne by the main north-south trunk road. All manner of vehicles are employed to carry goods and people from village to village and from town to town. There are bicycles ridden by spindly-legged boys, motor scooters by their elder brothers, horses and traps laden down with delicately-veiled young ladies, heavy wooden carts with oxen in harness, new Japanese saloon cars, garishly decorated buses with every one of their sixty seats full, and, last but not least, the long-haul heavy transports, lorries and trucks of all shapes and sizes, elaborately painted with imaginative landscapes and mythical beasts, and chromed to a dazzling and fantastic brightness.

*bove: Rhotas Fort, near Jhelum, is 109
lometres south of Rawalpindi. Built in the 1540s
y Sher Shah Suri, the fort was subsequently
xtended and developed by the Mughal Emperor
kbar. The walls, more than forty feet (twelve
etres) thick in places, enclose an area of 260
res.*

The lorry-drivers are, indisputably, the kings of the road in Pakistan. They are a self-contained, aristocratic fraternity and when one breaks down another will surely help him to get rolling again. They earn good money but work hard, long and often dangerous hours for it, clocking up prodigious feats of driving and endurance and covering vast distances with huge loads. All the bigger trucks carry a permanent staff of three—two drivers and a self-taught mechanic. While one driver presses on through the suffocating heat of the afternoon, when even the air at 110 kilometres an hour provides no cooling comfort, his assistant sleeps on the back seat or in a specially-constructed 'pocket' above the cab, ready to take on the gruelling eight-hour night-shift. The mechanic is on permanent standby and is expected to be able to cope with anything from a punctured tyre to a burnt-out piston-ring or a slipping clutch.

Anyone who journeys long enough and far enough in Pakistan will become aware that the roads have a life and a rhythm of their own. This special character is most easily seen in the many thousands of wayside rest-houses and eating stalls where, at any time of the day or night, the weary traveller can get a refreshing drink and a plate of savoury meats with chapatis—fried cakes of wholewheat flour.

The atmosphere of the rest-houses is timeless, reminiscent of the *serais* of Mughal times and of a rough homespun hospitality that the rest of the world has long forgotten how to offer. Here, if you are tired, you may stretch out and sleep for half an hour or half a day. Even the simplest rest-house will boast at least a dozen of the simple frame-beds known as *charpoys* (which means 'four legs') and it is most comforting to know that without formality or expense you may pull off the road and fling yourself down to rest. No one will question your right to be there and it is possible to enjoy a refreshing siesta on the taut string hammock of a *charpoy* with a gentle afternoon breeze blowing over you and the sun and the shade dappling down through the leaves and branches of the overarching trees.

Right: Rippled water of the Jhelum River casts back the shimmering reflections of the Jhelum Grand Mosque.

Above: Calm, radiant waters reflect the image of the Hiran Minar, or 'Deer Tower', built by Emperor Jehangir in memory of his pet antelope in 1607. The circular tower is 103 feet (31 metres) high.

When you awake from your doze, tea will be there if you need it, for the price of a few rupees. And this is not the insipid brew of the middle-class city suburb. The drink is made with fresh milk and strong brown leaves boiled up together with sugar into a stimulating syrup. Around you, as you drink, the life of the rest-house goes on, with lorry-drivers and travellers from all over the subcontinent exchanging news across the wooden dining-tables and calling their orders for food to the cook who squats above a firey charcoal oven, grilling kebabs and baking bread in the fragrant smoke-rich dusk.

The language of the road, and the national language of Pakistan, is Urdu. It unites all peoples and all communities, whatever their mother tongue. It is spoken as far north as Chitral, Gilgit and Skardu and as far south as Thatta and Karachi. The word *urdu* is of Turkish origin and means 'army' or 'camp' (the English word 'horde' has the same roots)—so *urdu* is, quite simply, the language of the camp. Scholars say that it developed in the Punjab and neighbouring territories about one thousand years ago out of an admixture of local languages and of the Persian spoken by invading armies from the north—a Persian that, incidentally, included many words borrowed from Arabic and Turkish.

Urdu is graceful and poetic with no over-harsh gutterals to cause a foreigner to stumble in his pronunciation. It is also a language that lends itself to scholarship and artistic endeavour and that rests on a vast and elegant body of literature and poetry going back some 700 years. Most notably, however, it is a polite and gentle language which, in its forms of speech, recognizes the basic equality of all humanity, bestowing equal respect on the servant and the master, the courtier and the king.

One of the places where the Urdu language grew up was the ancient city of Lahore which stands on the banks of the Ravi River about five hours' hard drive south of Rawalpindi by way of Jhelum, Gujrat and Gujranwala.

With a population of more than 2.5 million, Lahore is Pakistan's largest city after Karachi. It occupies a choice site in the midst of fertile alluvial plains. Ptolemy's *Geographia*, written about AD 150, refers to it as *Labokla* and locates it with reference to the Indus, the Ravi, the Jhelum and the Chenab rivers. The city next crops up in literature in connection with the campaigns of the Turkish dynast Mahmud of Ghazni against the Rajas of Lahore between 1001 and 1008. Around this time it established itself as the capital of the Punjab and thereafter began to play an important and growing rôle as a centre of Muslim power and influence in the subcontinent. Its heyday was the Mughal era from the early sixteenth century onwards and, as Mughal power

began to decline in the eighteenth and nineteenth centuries, Lahore suffered a concomitant period of ignominy and political eclipse. It was here, at the beginning of the nineteenth century, that the Sikh ruler Ranjit Singh declared himself Maharajah of the Punjab and allowed his troops to desecrate many of the city's beautiful Islamic shrines—including the Badshahi Mosque which was, for a while, converted into a powder magazine. By the time the British occupied Lahore in 1849, one writer was moved to describe the city as 'a mere expanse of crumbling ruins'.

The massive entrance of Badshahi Mosque (left) built by Emperor Aurangzeb in Lahore. The courtyard (above) is the largest in the world measuring 528 feet 8 inches (161.13 metres) by 528 feet 4 inches (161.03 metres). Up to 100,000 people pray here during open-air congregational meetings in the shadow of the four minarets, each 67 feet (20.4 metres) in circumference and 175 feet (53 metres) high.

Opposite: A nineteenth-century carved wooden door from Chiniot at the Mughal Gallery in Lahore Fort Museum.

Above: Brightly coloured mosaics on the inner wall of Lahore Fort depict scenes of battle and hunting.

Happily, this was an exaggeration and today the great buildings laid down by the long-vanished Mughal emperors may be seen in much of their original splendour. All the adverse influences since then seem to have been washed away, like sediment carried off by a flood, leaving behind the fundamental character and beauty of this old Islamic settlement. Fittingly, it was here in 1940 that the Muslim League made its first formal demand for the establishment of a Muslim homeland. A towering and graceful monument, the Minar-e-Pakistan now stands on the site of the passing of the Pakistan Resolution.

Nearby, the massively fortified walls of Lahore Fort speak eloquently of the centuries upon centuries of passing history that they have witnessed. The fort antedates the coming of Mahmud of Ghazni in the eleventh century, was ruined by the Mongols in 1241, rebuilt in 1267, destroyed again by Timurlane in 1398 and rebuilt once more in 1421. The great Mughal emperor Akbar replaced its mud walls with solid brick masonry in 1566 and extended it northwards. Later Jehangir, Shah Jehan and Aurangzeb all added the stamps of their widely differing personalities to its fortifications, gateways and palaces.

The fort encloses an area of approximately thirty acres and it is possible to spend many hours wandering there, lost in contemplation of times gone by, trying to reconstruct in your imagination a way of life that the world will never see again. The buildings within its walls are a testament to the gracious style of Mughal rule at its height, in which every man knew his place and courtly behaviour had been refined into an elaborately stratified social code. Much of the architecture reflects this code. From a raised balcony in the Diwan-e-Aam, or Hall of Public Audience, built by Shah Jehan in 1631, the emperors looked down on the common people over whom they ruled when they came to present petitions and to request the settlement of disputes. Wealthier citizens and the nobility were allowed to meet their emperors on a level floor in the Diwan-e-Khas—the Hall of Special Audience—which was also built by Shah Jehan, in 1633.

While the Halls of Audience are characterized by their strict functionality, other buildings raised under Shah Jehan's patronage are styled in a more imaginative and fanciful mood. Of these the Shish Mahal, or Palace of Mirrors, which stands on the fort's north side, is by far the most splendid. It consists of a row of high domed rooms, the roofs of which are decked out with hundreds of thousands of tiny mirrors in the fashion of the traditional Punjabi craft of *Shishgari* (designs made from mirror fragments). A fire-brand lit inside any part of the Palace of Mirrors throws back a million reflections that dizzy the eye and seem like a galaxy of far-off stars turning in an ink-blue firmament.

In the courtyard next to the Shish Mahal stands the Naulakha Pavilion, a building considered by scholars to be of major architectural importance. Viewed from without it is remarkable for its stark white marble-work and gracefully curving roof. Elaborately carved fretwork windows allow a refreshing breeze to blow into the Pavilion's single cool, bright room and out again through its five doors. The windows command a view over the walls of the fort to the streets and market-places beyond, and it is said that Mughal princesses used to sit here gazing out on the citizens of Lahore but unseen by them. Resting for a moment in the Pavilion from the heat and dust of the day and catching your reflection echoed endlessly in its thousand star-shaped mirrors, it is not difficult to imagine the tinkling distant laughter of these graceful, aristocratic, long-departed ladies.

Left: The Diwan-e-Aam (Hall of Public Audience), built by Shah Jehan in Lahore Fort in 1631, where the common people used to petition the Emperor and request the settlement of disputes.

Though Shah Jehan's 'Reign of Marble' gave the fort its most graceful
and architecturally accomplished buildings, his predecessor Jehangir
was also an active builder, laying down a complete palace with many
large and airy bedchambers arranged around a quadrangle. Jehangir,
the fourth of the great Mughals, is said to have had a special affection
for Lahore. According to a legend, before he ascended to the throne he
fell in love with a dancing girl here. Her name was Anarkali
('Pomegranate Blossom') and Jehangir, then simply Prince Salim,
determined to marry her. His father, the omnipotent Mughal Emperor
Akbar, ruler of the entire subcontinent, disagreed and forbade any
further contact between the high-born prince and the low-born dancer.
But still the dangerous love-affair continued. Akbar's response was
swift and uncharacteristically brutal. On his orders Anarkali was
entombed alive in a section of the wall of the old city of Lahore. For the
royal family, life went on much as before. Prince Salim suffered a severe
period of depression but recovered from it in time to take over the
throne from his father in 1605 and to adopt the name Jehangir, which
means 'world-conqueror'. He later married several wives, of whom the
most famous was the wise and artistic Nur Jehan ('Light of the World'),
but one wonders whether he ever really recovered from his poignant
and abruptly curtailed romance with the lovely Pomegranate Blossom.
Posterity at least has been kind to her. Near her tomb, Lahore's richest
and most colourful shopping area, the Anarkali Bazaar, is named after
her. In its maze of lanes and alley-ways decked out with shops and stalls
offering a fantastic range of traditional leatherware, embroidery, glass
bangles, silk dresses, and jewellery of beaten gold, it is possible to
recapture something of the gay spirit of the girl who gave her life for
love of a prince.

Jehangir established a reputation for justice, humanity and fair play
during his twenty-three years on the Mughal throne and, at the same
time, cultivated a pleasure-loving life given over to the enjoyment of
music and fine arts. In this respect he differed from Aurangzeb, the sixth
of the great Mughals, who believed that music and the pleasures of the
senses should have no place in Muslim society. Aurangzeb's tough,
uncompromising nature is reflected in the massive solidity of Lahore
Fort's Alamgiri gate which he built in 1674. Its frowning wooden door,

*Right: The Shish Mahal (Palace of Mirrors), a
magnificent edifice inside Lahore Fort, built as an
official residence for the Empress by Shah Jehan,
consists of a row of high-domed rooms, their roofs
decked out with thousands of tiny mirrors.*

centimetres thick, is studded with heavy iron nails put there to bloody the heads of elephants should an enemy have had the temerity to employ the huge beasts as living battering-rams.

The Alamgiri gate faces west. Opposite it, some two minutes' walk away across an open grassy square, stands the Badshahi Mosque, an even more potent symbol of Aurangzeb's towering personality. Its red sandstone courtyard, larger by far than any other place of worship in the Muslim world, measures an almost square 528 feet 8 inches by 528 feet 4 inches (161.13 metres by 161.03 metres). Up to 100,000 people can pray here during open-air congregational meetings in the shadow of four minarets, each 67 feet (20.4 metres) in circumference and 175 feet (53 metres) high.

But dimensions alone cannot convey the awesome solemnity of the Badshahi Mosque, or the sense of reverence it invokes. It was built, on Aurangzeb's command, in 1673–4 under the supervision of the Emperor's foster-brother Fadai Khan Koka. As if to contradict the massive scale of its construction, the architecture is gently and imaginatively crafted with arched gateways opening on to views of high marble domes. As a result, and despite the ravages that it suffered during the Sikh occupation of Lahore, the Badshahi Mosque endures today as a major example of Islamic architecture in its grandest and most creative mood.

Another magnificent remnant of the Mughal era, also partially vandalized in the late eighteenth century by the invading Sikhs, is the Shalimar Garden which stands on the Grand Trunk Road about eight kilometres to the east of the old part of Lahore. *Shalimar* means 'House of Joy' and, in truth, the passing centuries have done nothing to detract from the indefinable atmosphere of light-heartedness and laughter that characterizes this green and peaceful walled retreat. A canal runs the entire 2,006 foot (611 metres) length of the garden and from it 450 sparkling fountains throw up a skein of fresh water that cools and refreshes the atmosphere, making this a favourite place for afternoon walks for the citizens of modern Lahore.

Opposite: Lahore's bustling Anarkali Bazaar, teeming with shoppers in search of bargains, particularly leatherware, embroidered garments, glass bangles, beaten gold and silver jewellery, and silk cloths.

Opposite: Rich cloths for sale in Anarkali Bazaar, where deals often take hours to conclude as the seller details the virtues of his wares and the buyer focuses on their faults.

Right: Nan, the wholesome unleavened bread of the Punjab, on sale in Lahore. The dough is first patted into shape and then pushed through the hole at the baker's feet into a large spherical oven below, called a tandoor. About 4 feet deep, it is heated by a bed of charcoal. The dough, plastered to the oven wall, is removed with a long metal spike when ready.

The Shalimar, which covers an area of more than 40 acres, is divided into three successive terraces. The first terrace is called Farah Bakhsh (meaning 'refreshing') and the second and third terraces are called Faiz Bakhsh ('bountiful'). Construction of the garden was ordered by the Emperor Shah Jehan in 1641 and took seventeen months to complete to his satisfaction. Trees planted included mango, cherry, apricot, peach, plum, apple, almond, mulberry, orange, cypress and poplar. In 1711, some fifty years after Shah Jehan's death, it was reported that 128 staff were permanently employed in the upkeep of the gardens.

Fabled Shalimar Gardens of Lahore, built by Emperor Shah Jehan in 1641, are a favourite place for recreation (above). The gardens are divided into three terraces, covering an area of more than 40 acres. A canal runs the entire 2,006 foot (611 metres) length and 450 sparkling fountains (left) throw up a skein of fresh water to cool and refresh the atmosphere.

Overleaf: Emperor Jehangir's mausoleum stands in a beautiful 55-acre garden on the outskirts of Lahore. The mausoleum was built by Jehangir's son and successor, Shah Jehan.

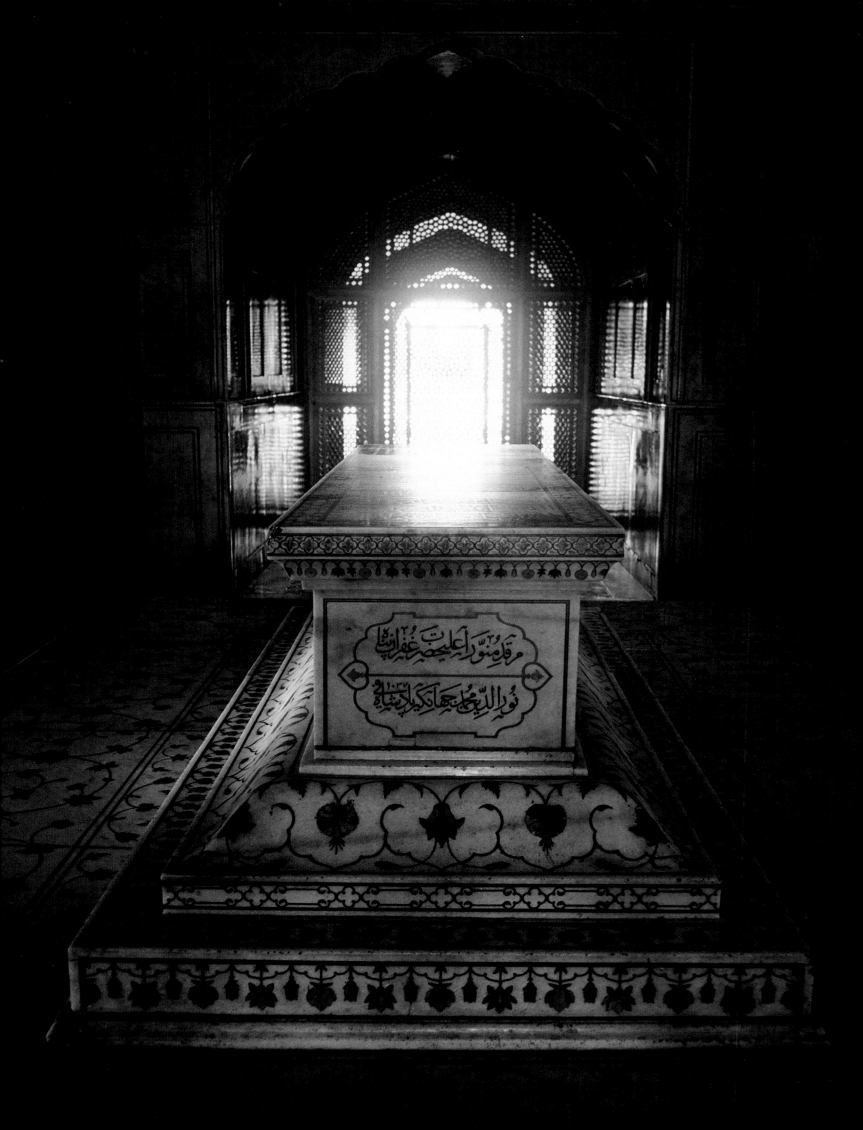

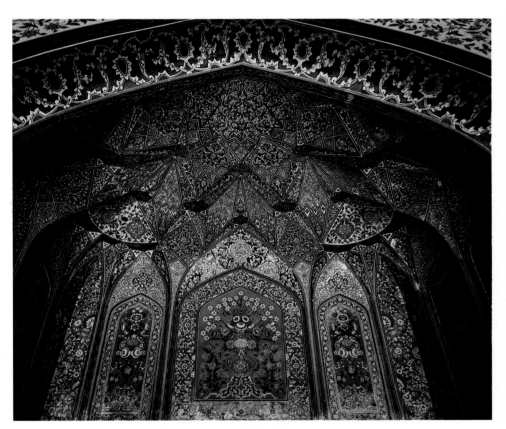

Opposite: Marble tomb of Jehangir built in 1633, engraved in beautiful Naskh script, giving 99 attributes of God.

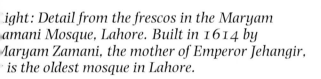

Right: Detail from the frescos in the Maryam Zamani Mosque, Lahore. Built in 1614 by Maryam Zamani, the mother of Emperor Jehangir, is the oldest mosque in Lahore.

Lahore is rightly regarded as the cultural, architectural and artistic centre of Pakistan; indeed, the city is so steeped in historical distinction that it would be possible to spend a lifetime studying it without learning everything that there is to learn. Lahore Museum, the oldest in Pakistan, is an education in itself. It tells the visitor much about the antiquity of the city and also of the surrounding countryside. The Museum stands on Lahore's most gracious street, the wide, tree-lined Mall. Outside it, like a sentinel guarding the treasures of the past, a massive muzzle-loading cannon is positioned. Called Zamzama, and immortalized by Kipling as Kim's Gun, it has a barrel 14 feet 4½ inches long and a bore of 9½ inches. It was cast in Lahore in 1757 from copper and brass, and is one of the largest pieces of ordnance ever produced in the subcontinent. The gun first saw action in 1761 at the Battle of Panipat and was subsequently used by Ranjit Singh in his campaigns. Persian verses inscribed on the barrel describe Zamzama as 'terrible as a dragon and huge as a mountain'.

Minaret of the Wazir Khan Mosque, Lahore, built in 1634 by Nawab Wazir Khan, a Viceroy of the Punjab under Emperor Shah Jehan. Famous for its mosaic work, the Mosque is regularly restored and renovated (bottom). The floral patterns are outstanding examples of the Persian school of variegated glazed tile and enamelled mosaic work depicting Quranic verses (right).

From a city so rich in artefacts and historical memorabilia as Lahore it is inevitably something of a culture-shock to venture out once more into the countryside. The main road runs in a south-westerly direction, roughly paralleling the course of the Ravi River, dotted with a string of small agricultural towns. Though this is a region of no outstanding natural beauty it has a pleasant tranquillity engendered by the endless kilometres of green rolling fields and the slow timeless toil of the farmers.

Away from the road with its hurtling lorries and loud-blowing horns you enter a world of villages. It is a world with different customs from those of the big cities of Pakistan, and very different rhythms; but it is also a world in which no one need feel himself a stranger for very long. The life-style is simple and uncluttered but not unprosperous. In the midst of bountiful crops of rice, wheat, tobacco, maize and cotton every family has enough to eat, every child has access to education, every man has work, and every woman can keep a dignified household.

The village of Malikabad, forty-eight kilometres south of Lahore, is not visible from the main road though it stands only a brisk twenty minutes' walk away from it amongst the varying shades of green of a plentiful harvest. Here some 2,000 souls grow enough staple crops to feed themselves throughout the year, supplementing their diet with milk, yoghurt and cheese produced by their herd of 1,000 buffaloes, 100 cows and 100 goats and sheep. Meat is regarded as something of a luxury and is usually bought on the special occasions when it is required with funds from the sale of surplus crops.

You enter Malikabad down a winding dusty path rutted with wheel-tracks left behind last rainy season by the village's heavy bullock-carts. From a doorway, two radiantly beautiful teenage girls dressed up in bright cotton dresses gaze out at you with frank puzzlement before bursting into a fit of giggles and retreating back into the shadows of their father's home. Like all the other women in the village they are unveiled and far less repressed and inhibited in their mannerisms than their stiff-necked urban cousins.

In the centre of the village, under a thatch-roofed shelter, several elders sit talking, each in his turn drawing pensively upon a bubbling hookah placed centrally on the ground in their midst. Without asking why you have come they invite you to join them as an honoured guest. Fearing that you will find the simple *charpoy* uncomfortable, a child is sent to fetch an armful of cushions. And, of course, because the afternoon is hot, you must have tea. The best china is produced and from a large pot on a separate tray is poured a thick, hot, mild and refreshing drink made from fresh buffalo's milk and sugar. It is pure ambrosia. No other tea you have ever had can compare with this tea. It banishes fatigue and relaxes the mind.

Left: Money garlands, popular in Pakistan, are used as gifts at ceremonial occasions and weddings. The most common garlands consist of one-rupee notes stapled to a cardboard base. In some cases, larger denominations are used.

Opposite: Pakistani bride, dressed in elegant finery, at her wedding in the town of Faisalabad. Weddings are amongst the most important ceremonial occasions in Pakistan.

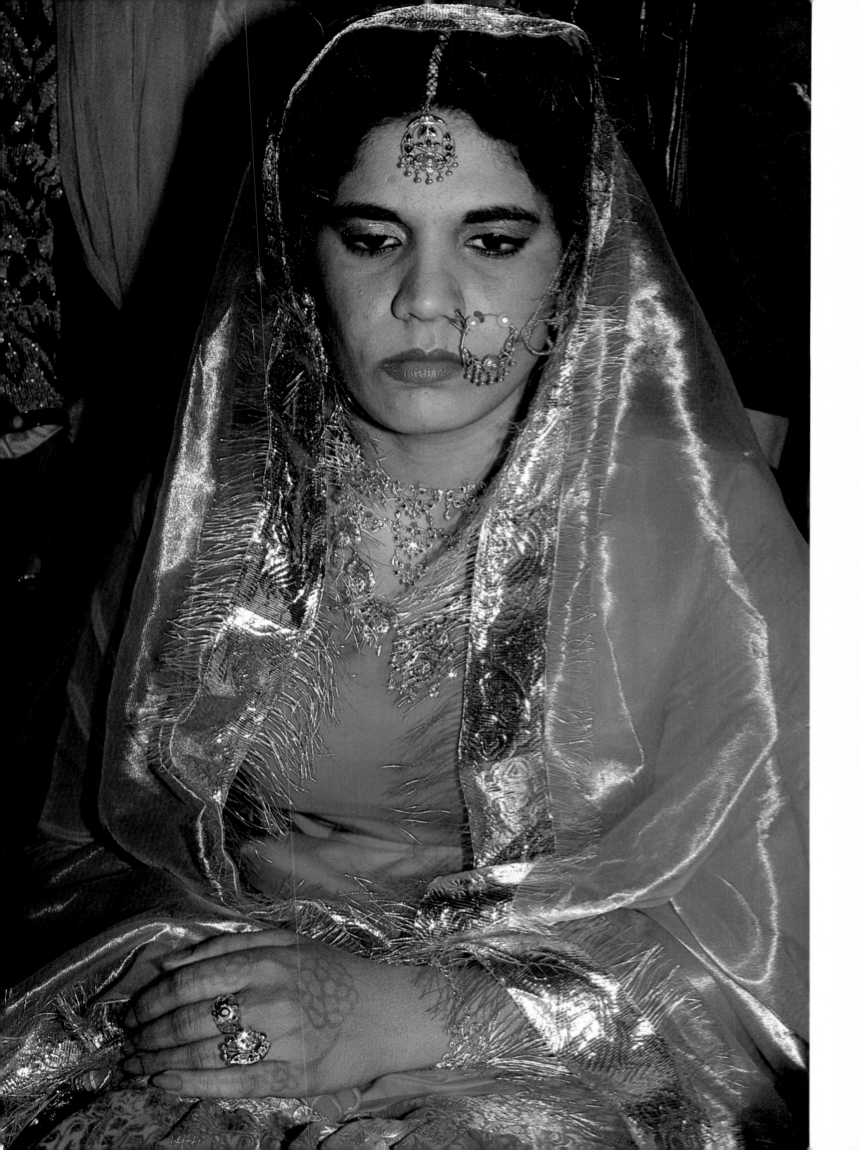

Time passes. Amongst the group of elders conversation moves back and forwards like the mouthpiece of the hookah. Your questions about the village, its crops and its people are answered and then met with other questions about yourself, your interests and your views. You have a sense of gradually and effortlessly getting to know these villagers and of the gradual and effortless way in which they are getting to know you. After a while they offer to show you around and, followed by a crowd of excited, curious children, you make your way from street to street.

Malikabad has a mosque and a small primary school of its own. The houses are, for the most part, made from mud strengthened with straw—although some of the larger dwellings have walls of burnt brick. There are three shops. Water, pumped from an artesian well, spreads outwards along well-formed irrigation channels, into the surrounding fields. Standing above the village, looking down on it from a raised grassy knoll, you are presented with an image of serene gentility. As you turn to go on your way, waving your farewells, you know that, however short your acquaintance, the hospitality and decency of these people is something that you will remember and cherish.

The maturity and self-confidence of the village people of central Pakistan is a reflection of the great antiquity of civilization in this region. About 160 kilometres to the south and west of Malikabad are to be found the ruins of Harappa, a city that flourished in the dawn of human history some 4,000 years ago. Harappa belonged to what archaeologists now call the Indus Valley Civilization and was linked to other long-dead cities strung out over 1,600 kilometres of Pakistan. The most famous of these was Moenjodaro, which stands in ruins some

Opposite: Hookah salesmen and their curiously-shaped wares in Bahawalpur market. The hookah, a popular means of smoking tobacco in Pakistan, is used at many social gatherings.

Above: Ornate patterns decorate a beautiful cotton rug woven in Bahawalpur. Although equipment is simple, the work of these craftsmen endures many years.

Opposite: On board his boat, a Sindhi sailor smokes a hookah, seated on a charpoy, a simple string bed.

1,280 kilometres south of Harappa on the west bank of the Indus, in modern Sind Province.

Excavations at Harappa and Moenjodaro began in 1921 and 1922 and quickly put paid to the then prevailing notion that Pakistan of the third and second millennia BC had been inhabited only by primitive nomadic tribes. The twin cities are remarkable for their well-constructed covered drainage systems, for their orderly parallel streets, and for their use of advanced building materials and techniques. Their layouts suggest that they were designed purposefully by master architects and city planners, while the discovery within them of polished stone weights and measures suggests the existence of stringently codified civic regulations.

Piecing together the past from shards of pottery, steatite seals, clay figurines, and the ruins of burnt-brick houses, is an unsatisfying and necessarily inconclusive task. But these are the only raw materials that the passing years have left us in Harappa and Moenjodaro. The picture that emerges from the work that has been done is of an orderly, hierarchical and prosperous society more concerned with the comforts

Below: Camel nomad sits proudly astride his elaborate saddle in Bahawalpur. A significant minority of Pakistan's 84 million people are nomads, living mainly in the provinces of Baluchistan and Sind. Camels are common throughout much of the country.

Below: Making ornaments from treated and painted camel skin is a typical Multani craft. Malik Mohammed Ashiq Naqqash puts the finishing touches to a vase in his shop in the Hussain Agahi Bazaar.

of life than with raising any great or glorious monuments to forgotten deities. Such religion as there was apparently revolved around a 'mother goddess' cult, common also to ancient Iraq and to the early Nile civilizations of Egypt. In both Harappa and Moenjodaro numerous terracotta figurines depicting the mother goddess have been unearthed. They display broad hips, large breasts and a peaky, full-lipped face with bulging eyes.

The standard of workmanship put into these figurines was not very high—however, this does not mean that the Harappans were unaccomplished at carving and sculpture. Several realistic and beautifully formed limestone statues of the human form have been found and there is the sensitively crafted and aesthetically pleasing 'dancing girl' in bronze—a slim, naked child with hips swung as though in time to a drum rhythm. One of the best-known pieces is a bearded, frowning bust from Moenjodaro referred to by archaeologists as the 'King Priest'. It is supposed that while the individual cities enjoyed a great deal of autonomy there was an overall federal structure to the Indus Valley Civilization in which a small aristocracy held absolute power of life and death over the mass of the populace. Perhaps this sneering, aloof and somehow cruel-looking figure depicts one of the ruling class, a high-born noble before whom others bowed in terror.

Other statues, carvings and figurines from Harappa and Moenjodaro tell us that, during the era in which civilization in these cities was at its height, the environment of the Indus Valley was very different from today. Creatures frequently depicted include many that only live in or near tropical forests, such as water buffalo and tiger. Crocodiles, elephants and rhinoceroses, long gone from these regions, are also shown in great abundance.

Harappa and Moenjodaro rose out of the mists of pre-history around 2500 BC. They collapsed just as suddenly about one thousand years later. The reasons for the demise of this unusual civilization are not fully understood. Though many examples of the pictographic script used in Harappa and Moenjodaro exist, all attempts to decipher the language of the ancient Indus Valley have proved fruitless, so there is no written record to guide us. The best guess is that Sanskrit-speaking Aryans, who invaded the subcontinent from the north in successive waves around 1500 BC, sacked the twin cities and destroyed the agricultural base on which their wealth rested. It also seems likely that, by this time, the citizens of Harappa and Moenjodaro had become lazy and decadent and that, as a result, their society had begun to decay from within. Although a number of the human remains found at Moenjodaro and Harappa show signs of a violent end, they do not exist in great enough numbers to suggest a massacre. Neither is there much evidence of weaponry. Perhaps the rich, mercantile and essentially unwarlike citizens simply ran away before the rampaging barbarians from the north. We shall probably never know the answer and, in a way, the atmosphere of unsolved mystery and hidden secrets that hangs over the ruins adds to their interest and to their romance.

Left: Ancient ruins of Harappa, a once-great city of the Indus Valley Civilization which flourished more than 4,500 years ago. Harappa was linked to Moenjodaro, some 1,280 kilometres to the south and there is evidence the two cities traded with ancient Egypt. Steatite seals (below), found in Harappa, bear ancient writing and also depict unicorns and bulls. It consists of formal pictorial symbols, written from left to right.

Opposite: Tomb of the famous saint Shah Rukn-e-Alam, in Multan. Pilgrims walk several times around the tomb, pausing to touch its four corners and whisper prayers. The exterior is decorated with glazed tile patterns, string courses and battlements, and was built in 1320.

Above: In Multan's Hussain Agahi Bazaar an artist puts the finishing touches to a superb blue china plate.

Previous pages: The great bath at Moenjodaro. Since many of the homes excavated in this 4,500-year-old city have private baths, archaeologists assume it was used for ceremonial or religious purposes. In the background is a Buddhist stupa built about 2,000 years ago with stones from the ruined city.

Harappa stands just off the main road some 184 kilometres from Lahore. Two hours' drive further on, continuing in a south-westerly direction, is Multan—a city that was born only a few hundred years after the Indus Valley Civilization died and that has endured into the twentieth century with all its vitality and ancient wisdom intact.

Multan has a unique climate characterized by frequent rainstorms, thunder and lightning, suffocating tropical heat, and dust. As a 300-year-old Persian couplet sums up:

With four things rare Multan abounds,
Dust, beggars, heat and burial grounds.

These days of course, the beggars are few; but no one can quarrel with the description of Multan as a city of burial-grounds. Here more tombs are to be found gathered together in one place than anywhere else in Pakistan, and the city is dominated by the towering brick and marble shrine of its eleventh-century patron saint, Shah Rukn-e-Alam.

The sixty foot (eighteen metre) high octagonal shrine stands within the walls of Multan Fort and is an object of veneration for Muslims not only from Pakistan but also from neighbouring countries. It is set in the midst of a broad tiled courtyard, and its most distinctive feature is its massive blue and white dome. From soon after dawn until just before nightfall the tomb receives an unbroken stream of visitors who come to leave fresh-cut flowers and to say their devotions, in the belief that by so doing they will be brought closer to God. For Muslim and non-Muslim alike it is a profoundly moving experience to stand inside the shrine in the cool, still air beneath the arching roof soaring away upwards into shadow. To watch the pilgrims is to share their mood of reverence. Many walk several times around the tomb of the saint, pausing to touch its four corners and to whisper prayers. Others simply sit in silence, lost in contemplation. When they depart they walk out backwards, facing the tomb, their eyes cast down in the manner of supplicants before a great king.

Multan is steeped in the Islamic faith, which has been the dominant influence here since the young Arab General Mohamed Bin Qasim made it his forward base in the subcontinent after conquering Sind in the early eighth century. The city flourished during the Mughal era, becoming famous for its musicians and for the skill of its craftsmen who perfected a special style of blue and white glazed tilework and delicate hand-painted vases and plates. Later, during the decline of the Mughals in the eighteenth century, when the subcontinent was subjected to numerous invasions and competing tyrannies, Multan continued to enjoy prosperity. The city's fortunes, however, like those of Lahore, took a temporary downward turn when the Sikhs seized power in the Punjab at the beginning of the nineteenth century. Noting that 'religious persecution is always revolting, and exercises a baneful influence in every age and country,' Alexander Burnes, a Scottish adventurer who journeyed up the Indus in 1831, observed of Multan: 'In this city, which held for upwards of 800 years so high a Mahommedan supremacy, there is now no public "numaz"; the true believer dare not lift his voice in public. The "Eeds" and the "Mohurum" pass without the usual observances; the "Ullaho Acbar" of the priest is never heard; the mosques are yet frequented but the pious are reduced to offering up their orisons in silence.'

Left: Holiday-makers negotiate the water-lilies in Lal Suhanra Lake, Bahawalpur National Park.

Today Multan has recovered its Islamic character, as any visitor to the city's well-attended congregational mosque can affirm. During Friday prayers the open tree-lined courtyard is full to overflowing, while at other times visitors come here simply to rest in the pleasant shade by the reflecting pool. Some read the Quran, others gather in little groups to talk in hushed voices about the affairs of the day. It is not unusual to see an old man come in off the street in order to lie down and sleep, and children are equally welcome here, dancing and skipping through patches of sunlight into the cool interior of the mosque. Islam's great strength is that it is the religion of the common man and of everyday life. It does not seek to separate itself from ordinary experience or to carve a specially privileged niche for itself in society. No high priests stand between the individual and his God. There are no complicated rituals to be monopolized by a rich and powerful élite.

The 'everyday' character of Islam is very much in evidence in the streets of the oldest part of Multan near the Hussain Agahi Bazaar. Here tiny mosques built into the city walls are interspersed with the shops of tradesmen, and people pray between a stall selling grilled meats and the brightly-coloured wares of a dye vendor. Hussain Agahi ranks amongst the most fascinating bazaars in the world, combining all the intrigue and cunning of an ancient Arab *souk* with the boisterous charm and pungent aromas of the subcontinent. Although the traditional goods of the market are now sold alongside transistor radios, colour televisions and spare parts for automobiles and motor bikes, it is still possible to get at least a partial glimpse of what Multan must have been like five hundred or even one thousand years ago.

To complete the picture it is only necessary to step off the bazaar's main street into the warren of alley-ways surrounding it on every side. Here tall houses of great antiquity throng together, their steep roofs and trellised wooden balconies almost touching above the narrow cobblestone lanes. It is as though you have been transported suddenly and abruptly back in time, to the Middle Ages or beyond. Behind you, in the early evening, fluorescent lights glow and car engines throw up their familiar din; ahead of you is another world where the twentieth century does not intrude. As you penetrate this world you find yourself gradually falling under its spell, staring in fascination into the broad courtyards that you stumble across, where ragged children play by firelight amongst slumbering buffalo. Losing all sense of direction you call for someone to guide you and a child takes your hand. You walk together silently, picking your way across the open drains that run parallel to the streets and marvelling at the degree to which the cobblestones have been worn down by the passing tread of unknown people over countless years. In a moment you emerge again on to a main road more than a kilometre away from your point of entry into

Right: Ancient tomb of Bibi Jawindi built in the city of Uchchh Sharif in 1494, stands on a hill overlooking a fertile valley.

Left and above: The courtyard and elaborate prayer hall of the Grand Mosque at Bhong, near Sadiqabad in the Punjab. As a young man its builder had a vision in which he was told that he would live as long as he continued to build the mosque. Construction finally stopped when he was well into his 80s and he died a month later.

*Above: The curious sabot-shaped, wooden house-
boats of the Indus fisherfolk moored against the
river bank at Sukkur. Many of the boats are old,
having been passed on from father to son through
several generations.*

Old Multan and, without a word, your guide leaves you, flitting back into the silent shadows of the incomprehensible past.

Multan is a complex and multi-layered city that combines a strong and fascinating flavour of age with a thrusting modernism and business acumen. Several large textile mills and cotton ginneries are situated here as well as a foundry, a fertilizer factory and an oil refinery. The city is also an important market-place for the agricultural produce of the lower Punjab, an area of great fertility due to the plentiful availability of water.

About one hundred kilometres south of Multan the rivers of the Punjab finally join in a green triangle of land known as the Panjnad. Out of the triangle one mighty river emerges, the Indus, to roll ponderously through the semi-desert province of Sind towards the sea, still some 800 kilometres away. The province is named after the river which also once lent its name to the whole subcontinent.

The ruins of Moenjodaro bespeak the tremendous age of human civilization in Sind but the first written records of the region relate to the invasion of Alexander the Great in 325 BC. Alexander was seriously injured in a battle with fierce tribesmen outside Multan but after his recovery he proceeded on down the Jhelum and Indus Rivers with a fleet of about 2,000 ships, capturing and securing Sukkur and the surrounding territory. Eventually, he made his way to the sea—thence to sail for home—at a place that the historians call Alexander's Haven, which was probably somewhere in the region of modern Karachi.

The first major town that the traveller who follows Alexander's historic route into Sind will come to is Sukkur, some seven hours' drive to the south-west of Multan. Its character is moulded around the river that flows through it, on which high-rigged, sabot-shaped boats ply slowly to and fro across the current. Here, in the shadow of the Grand Mosque, which casts the reflections of its shimmering minarets on the waters of the Indus, fisherfolk and river people lead proud and independent outdoor lives, exposed to the elements and to the vicissitudes of nature.

Their settlements are strung out in a ragged line along the river banks, thatched wooden huts on shore and huge, leaking houseboats afloat on the water. The fishermen's tough looks, gaudy ear-rings and unruly hair seem to be the hallmarks of latter-day pirates yet, on closer acquaintance, they emerge as gentle, kind-hearted people with a delightful wry sense of humour and a calm and stoical fatalism. Pausing to smoke a home-rolled cigarette with them and to drink a cup of tea you are aware of the beauty of the river in the early morning as little unhurried wavelets lap against the mud embankment. The shouts of children bathing far away in mid-stream carry effortlessly across the still sunny air and mingle with the rhythm of clothes being slapped dry by a laundryman against the flat black rock.

Turning south from Sukkur the road runs straight and true through some of the more fertile regions of Sind. Cultivation here is plentiful but, in the absence of effective irrigation, depends to a great extent on the moods of the Indus. Though the river flows sluggishly for most of the year it has a tendency to flood—a tendency that is the basis for more than 40 per cent of Sind's agriculture. Over the millenn... ...has deposited so much alluvium along its path that in man... banks and even its bed are above the level of the surrou... This is why it is capable of inundating very extensive a... countryside but it is also why the river has come to be... temperamental and sometimes dangerous ally by the... close proximity to it. Unconstrained by mountains or... valley walls, it has changed its course suddenly and c... times over the last five centuries.

One such change of course dramatically improved... Hyderabad, some 320 kilometres to the south of Suk... eighteenth century. Hyderabad was then known as... Indus flowed peacefully enough to the east of it. In... unpredictable river flexed its muscles and shifted int... the west of the town. A few years later, because of th... south that had resulted from the change of course, S... saintly Ghulam Shah Kalhora, moved his capital to... same time renaming it Hyderabad. In 1768, to mar... the town and to render it more easily defensible, he... to vacate its old dried mud fortress and to begin wo... structure of burnt brick. This fort, built in less than... foundation stone which bears the inscription 'O Go... city'. But Hyderabad was to see its fair share of war... in 1773 and was buried in an imposing mausoleun... fort. Ten years after his death the Kalhora family w... the Talpur dynasty, which originated in Baluchista... than half a century later the Talpurs were overthro... after a violent and bloody war, by the invading Briti...

Left: Interior of the Grand Mosque at Sukkur, traditional capital of Sind Province on the west bank of the Indus.

Above: Sindhi youths wearing hats typical of the
province.

The oval fort built by Ghulam Shah still stands today, in the centre of modern Hyderabad, and bears very little evidence of the skirmishes that have taken place outside the one-kilometre circumference of its walls. Around them, traffic moves ceaselessly. Horse-drawn carts mingle with more elaborate six-seater landaus. A whole local industry is given over to carriage-making and the craftsmen are renowned for their painstaking attention to detail. It is an absorbing experience to watch a master at work embossing a huge wooden wheel with bright nails and chrome, or carving intricate designs into the tailboard of a landau.

The route out of Hyderabad at first takes you westwards, crossing the Indus at Kotri on a huge combined road-and-rail bridge about 400 yards (365 metres) long. Here, on the banks of the river, water-melons are cultivated in great abundance as they have been since time immemorial. It is interesting that the Spanish word for water-melon, *sandia*, is a colloquial adaptation of 'Sind'. The fruit was originally brought from here to Spain more than one thousand years ago when the Arabs ruled over an empire that stretched from the Indian Ocean to the western Mediterranean.

After Kotri, the road turns southwards, still following the Indus. To the east the land stretches away green and fertile, well-irrigated by canals and providing a favourable environment for such crops as wheat, cotton and tobacco. The southern route, however, quickly brings you to a flat, monotonous, sandy desert. This is the Sind which one writer has described as a land of many silences: 'Silence of the desert and the immensity of light without shade; silence as of drowsy forenoon of those peaceful stretches of the river that have no allurement for the fisher; silence more solemn of the dreary wastes where the river joins the sea on a lonely coast.' It is also the Sind of mystics and saints whose bones now lie interred within its earth beneath a multitude of tombs. And it is the Sind of great and gifted poets like Shah Abdul Latif who in the early eighteenth century wrote:

All speak of the open path,
I want one who suggests the complex one.
Go not near the open road,
Seek after the complex one,
Suffer tribulation and come out raimentless.

Only rare ones enter the complex path;
The abode of the beloved is confusion for men,
They that walk the wilds
Are never misled;
Who walk the open road
Get plundered on the way.

Opposite: Crowded Hyderabad market-place with vintage 1914 clock tower in background.

Opposite: Famous craftsman Moharam Gill Mohammad, at work on his potter's wheel in Hala, near Hyderabad.

Right: Carpenter at Hyderabad ornaments wheel hub of a bullock-cart with metal studs. Pakistanis like colourful decorations on their vehicles.

Some ninety-six kilometres to the south of Hyderabad on the National Highway is the ancient town of Thatta, with its rich echoes of Sind's distinguished past. One of the mysteries of the empty, silent zone in which Thatta stands is that it was once fertile and prosperous, plentifully peopled, and connected by trading links to distant countries. The city itself is more than 2,000 years old. It was at Thatta that Alexander the Great rested his weary troops after their long and dusty journey from the north while his admiral Nearchus assembled his fleet at the apex of the Indus delta 'to lead it down the tortuous channels of uncharted waters of the great river Indus to the sea.' In more recent times Thatta enjoyed the high patronage of the Mughal emperors of the subcontinent. Nearby in the Makli Hills, tombs of the Mughal nobility are to be found intermingled with hundreds of thousands of graves from earlier and later eras in a vast necropolis that extends over an area of fifteen square kilometres. Perhaps the best-preserved monument is the tomb of Issa Khan Tarkhan, governor of Thatta during the reign of Emperor Shah Jehan. It consists of a square tomb-chamber which is carved up to the dome and surrounded by a two-storeyed pillared verandah. The main structure and the enclosure walls are profusely decorated with richly-carved surface tracery.

Shah Jehan had a special affection for Thatta. During the struggle for succession that followed the death of his father Jehangir, Shah Jehan briefly took refuge in Sind and was treated with great kindness and hospitality. In later life, as a gesture of gratitude, he ordered the building of a mosque in Thatta. Now known as the Shah Jehan Mosque, it is a splendid example of Muslim architecture, admired for its glazed tilework and symmetrical arches painted with floral patterns.

Why should a city once so rich, which acted as a magnet for the great and the powerful in former times, have been reduced today to little more than a provincial town of narrow undistinguished alley-ways between brick and adobe buildings? The answer is the Indus, whose changing course elevated Hyderabad from anonymity to the rank of the third-largest city in Pakistan.

Opposite: The tomb of Lal Shahbaz, the patron saint of Sind, at Sewan Sharif.

Opposite: Colourfully-clothed Sindhi family.

Below: Cobras rise and sway to the music of the snake-charmers in Thatta. Snake venom sacs are usually removed and the skill of charming is handed down from generation to generation.

Left: Thatta's ancient burial ground on Makli Hills, largest necropolis in the world, where many of the graves are adorned with Quranic inscriptions.

Above: Tombs of nobles stand alongside graves of hundreds of thousands of ordinary people from earlier and later years in the vast necropolis at Makli Hills which extends over an area of 15 square kilometres. Exquisitely carved sandstone monuments are a feature of this site. The carvings differentiate between males and females: knights on horseback indicate a man's grave; a woman's grave is indicated by jewellery.

Thatta's prosperity was based on its rôle as a busy river port. In the early eighteenth century, according to one visitor, more than 40,000 vessels plied for hire here and the countryside around was 'very fruitful and pleasant . . . rich and fertile almost as covetousness could wish'. The effects of silting of the river channel to the sea and a gradual eastward swing of the main body of the Indus, however, brought an end to Thatta's greatness. In the mid-nineteenth century an English traveller walked down long streets of uninhabited houses and reported his disappointment at finding the city's glory 'completely departed' and its appearance 'ruined and deserted'.

Thatta was not the only victim of the geographical forces at play in the broad sweep of the Indus delta. At nearby Bhanbore the remains of another once-busy port dating back to the first century BC have been discovered. Archaeologists identify the site with the ancient city of Debul stormed and captured by Mohamed Bin Qasim in 711, at the beginning of the campaign that made Sind the first home of the Islamic faith in the subcontinent. The remains of what is almost certainly the earliest mosque in South Asia have been found here, bearing an inscription that gives the date of construction as 727.

The River Indus buries its past as it makes its future. Bhanbore, in all its sublime antiquity, lies a bare sixty-four kilometres from Karachi, the brash historical upstart that is modern Pakistan's largest, richest and most energetic city.

Opposite: Symmetrical archways in the Shah Jehan Mosque at Thatta. The Mosque was built by the Mughal Emperor Shah Jehan out of gratitude for the hospitality shown to him in Sind during the struggle for succession that followed his father's death. It is a splendid example of Islamic architecture.

Overleaf: Karachi skyline, with the towering Habib Bank Plaza shaped like a column of coins. Karachi is the commercial capital of Pakistan.

Chapter Four   The City and the Desert

Karachi enjoys a splendid natural harbour, one of the best in the subcontinent. It has only seriously exploited this valuable asset in the last hundred years although its potential for great prosperity was visible somewhat earlier. 'You will yet be the glory of the East,' prophesied Sir Charles Napier, the British General who conquered Sind. 'Would that I could come again, Karachi, to see you in your grandeur.' Napier's first visit was in 1843, when the great city was an insignificant and unappealing coastal town with a population of, at most, a few thousands. Called Kullachi, it had two gates, Mithadar, facing a sweet water well, and Kharadar, facing the salty sea. Today, though the walled nineteenth-century town is long gone, its 'sweet' and 'salt' gates are remembered in the names of two of Karachi's oldest neighbourhoods. In one of them, Mithadar, the founder of Pakistan, Quaid-i-Azam Mohammad Ali Jinnah, was born on 25 December 1876.

Fifty years after the arrival of the British, who built a military cantonment here, Karachi's population was still only 60,000. However, some of the main features of the modern city had been laid down, including the Bohri Bazaar, Saddar Bazaar and Empress Market—still Karachi's luxury shopping-area. Business had also been growing steadily. In 1843–4 the total value of the city's trade was just US $244,320. Ten years later the figure had risen to US $1,770,206 and, by 1860, it had risen again to US $5,367,300. Thereafter the rate of growth quickened dramatically and, by the beginning of the twentieth century, Karachi was worth over US $20 million a year.

In 1947 the new state of Pakistan was born and Karachi was established as its capital. The city had by then a population of 400,000 but, with the new rôle and importance bestowed on it by Independence, business boomed and there was a massive influx of immigrants from all over the country and from India in search of jobs. Just twenty years later Karachi's population topped the two million mark and, by 1981, stood at almost six million with no obvious sign of a slow-down in its rate of growth. Though Karachi is no longer Pakistan's capital, having surrendered that honour to Islamabad in 1959, its dominance in the national economy is beyond dispute. The port handles some 15 billion tonnes of cargo annually and is one of the most important shipping-centres in south Asia. Karachi is also the main terminus of Pakistan's railway system and the site of the principal international airport. About one quarter of the country's industry is located here.

Karachi's charm is hard to define. At one level it is a harsh mercantile city with all the brash, skin-deep self-assurance of the *nouveau riche*; at another level its complex, colourful bazaars bespeak an ancient oriental tradition of barter and exchange; at still another level it is the most advanced city in Pakistan, boasting advanced educational institutions, a nuclear power-station and sophisticated banking and

Opposite: Sunset over Karachi harbour, Pakistan's largest and busiest port.

Below: Attractive ceramics enhance the Masjid-e-Tooba, also known as Defence Society Mosque, elegantly designed by a Pakistani architect, Dr Babet Hamid. The mosque was built with donation from the Armed Forces at the cost of 4.5 million rupees in 1969.

technical skills. At certain times of day its busy streets become so clogged with traffic that all movement stops and the air is filled with exhaust fumes and a nerve-jangling symphony of horn blasts. At other times, in the early morning and evening, it is possible to enjoy a walk along the wide, sweeping, tree-lined boulevards and to sense amongst them faint echoes of a less frenetic era. Most of all, beneath its ever-changing skyline littered with tall cranes and the red girders of construction, Karachi is a city of contrasts that reflect the many-sided

Below: Vessels berthed alongside a wharf in Karachi, one of the most important ports in south Asia, handling 15 billion tonnes of cargo a year.

complexity of Pakistan itself. Here camel-carts and pick-up trucks go side by side and camel-caravans, sprinkled with the red dust of the long southward trek through Baluchistan, compete for road space with ten-ton lorries. In Karachi's harbour Japanese-built oil tankers and Arab dhows share the same stretches of oily water. And in the markets, millionaires who have not yet bothered to change their bare feet and ragged clothes for more elegant apparel are to be found haggling over the price of a bale of cloth.

Karachi's cloth bazaar is in fact an excellent place to sample for the first time the intoxicating atmosphere of this great city. Here amidst the food- and drink-stalls that seem to congregate wherever goods are bought and sold, merchants from all over Pakistan are to be found engaged in the serious business of making money. Textiles are still the country's largest industry and Karachi is the largest wholesale centre for the products of this industry—products which are then moved to retail outlets as far away as Peshawar and Rawalpindi, Quetta and Lahore.

Negotiating the streets of the cloth-market calls for certain skills. There is little pleasure in driving through the narrow cramped spaces between the tall brick houses. The pedestrian must be constantly on the lookout for motor scooters and *jintneys* which whizz to and fro with scant respect for anyone who gets in their path. The din of horns and bicycle-bells mingles excitingly with the coarse cries of the traders and the shouts of the coolies demanding right of way for their hand-pushed barrows laden down with bundles of cloth.

The main business of the bazaar is not done in the open air. Up steep flights of stone steps haggard accountants sit in gloomy offices doing complicated sums on noisy electric calculators. Here too, traditionally, tax lawyers have their offices and provide an on-the-doorstep service to the rag-trade millionaires.

The actual business of buying and selling of cloth is done at ground-level in large covered halls where broad-bladed fans stir the thick air without cooling it. Merchants and customers sit cross-legged amongst the multi-coloured wares, their sandals thrown down carelessly on the concrete floor of the thoroughfare amongst star-shaped slaps of spat-out betel-juice. There is a subdued hum of conversation occasionally broken by loud guffaws of laughter as a deal is struck. Piles of hundred-rupee notes change hands as though money were going out of fashion.

Karachi is a city of many markets; indeed, in a sense, the whole city is one large market. The main shopping areas for general purchases are strung along M. A. Jinnah Road, Abdullah Haroon Road, Tariq Road and Zeb-un-Nisa Street. Here magnificent hand-woven carpets can be found and cheap glass bangles and other trinkets vie for shop-window space with the best in gold and silver jewellery. Numerous restaurants offer a pleasing variety of Pakistani, European and Chinese cuisine, but one of the delights of Karachi is the simple savoury fare that can be purchased from stall-holders by the roadside. Kebabs and nehari, a spicy meat and gravy dish, are specialities, and sticky sweet cakes and confections called halwa are also worth sampling.

Karachi Museum is a major repository of national treasures and a centre of archaeological and historical research. Situated in the heart of the city in pleasant gardens, it is divided into a Pre-historic Gallery, a Buddhist-Hindu Gallery, a Muslim Gallery, an Ethnological Gallery, a

*Above: Fishermen on Keenjhar Lake, 125
kilometres north of Karachi. The biggest man-made
lake in Pakistan, Keenjhar is rich with fish.*

Manuscripts Hall and numismatics section. The Muslim Gallery contains a particularly fine collection of miniature paintings, an art-form that was in high vogue during the Mughal era. The realistic portrayal of court scenes and of emperors and empresses helps to bring to life this chivalrous period in Pakistan's history. The Manuscripts Hall features a number of extremely ancient copies of the Holy Quran, illuminated throughout and characterized by delicate and imaginative calligraphy.

Because it is relatively new, the city of Karachi is not rich in ancient monuments and shrines like Lahore and Multan. It is here, however, that Quaid-i-Azam Mohammad Ali Jinnah is laid to rest, and his mausoleum is regarded as an outstanding example of modern Islamic architecture. It is built entirely of white marble, with impressive arches in the North African style. Standing in the midst of a green and flowery lawn it has a unique air of serene solemnity.

Karachi is an ideal centre for exploring the surrounding countryside which, as well as places of historical interest like Thatta and Bhanbore, features the Kirthar National Park and Haleji, Keenjhar and Manchar Lakes. Haleji, located between Bhanbore and Thatta about eighty-eight kilometres from Karachi, is the country's principal bird sanctuary and the winter home of many migratory species. Keenjhar, 125 kilometres from Karachi, is famous for its fish and is the largest man-made lake in Pakistan. Lake Manchar covers an area of 253 square kilometres but is never more than five metres deep. It is home to some 2,000 fishermen whose life-style has, in many respects, remained unchanged for hundreds of years. While visiting sportsmen knock ducks out of the sky with 12-gauge shotguns, the Manchar fisherfolk adhere to an older and more resourceful method of catching their dinner. The hunter bores peep holes in a large earthenware jar and draws it over his head like a diver's helmet. He then immerses himself in the lake and swims slowly and noiselessly towards the unsuspecting ducks sitting on the water. They pay no attention to just one more piece of floating debris which is all the hunter looks like. Once in the midst of the flock all he has to do is reach out with both hands and grab a brace of birds.

Of course, Karachi is a fine holiday resort in its own right and many visitors to Pakistan never venture beyond its boundaries. The city enjoys year-round sunshine and has extensive facilities for yachting, sailing, skin-diving, tennis, squash, polo and other games and sports. There are also a number of white-sand beaches within striking distance, lapped by the warm waters of the Arabian Sea. Hawkes Bay, the Sandspit and Paradise Point are the least spoiled and most accessible, and Gadiani Beach, further to the west, is also worth a visit. Clifton Beach, six and a half kilometres from the centre of town, stretches in a south-easterly direction and is a popular weekend resort. Although sections of it have been polluted by the hundreds of ships that

Opposite: Sunset over Lake Manchar brings a mood of quiet reflection. The lake, which covers an area of 253 square kilometres, is never more than 16 feet (5 metres) deep.

stand off Karachi Harbour waiting in the queue to unload their cargoes, this is still a scenic and even a romantic spot. In the early evening there are dramatic views of the city skyline, which takes on a warm glow against the night sky as lights appear in every window. The sun sinks quickly, colouring the waves blood red before it slips behind the horizon, silhouetting a distant dhow with its sails fully extended. This was the sea that Sindbad sailed and that the Arabs crossed to bring their hard and pure religion to the subcontinent.

As night falls, and a cooling breeze billows in across the lapping waters, the crowds strolling amongst the food-stalls begin to thin out and the brightly bedecked camels that have been giving rides all day to giggling children are released from harness and led away to graze. Only in the Clifton East Amusement Park does the fairground atmosphere persist for a few hours longer. Amidst the neon and the chrome, the Waltzer takes excited teenagers on spinning, noisy, centrifugal journeys and the loud refrain of transistorized music mingles with the crash and hum of the dodgem cars. One has a sense of the vitality of urban life and of the huge social and economic power of the myriads of people who work and pray and raise their families here. It is easy to forget that Karachi is surrounded by the vast empty spaces of the sea and the desert.

Pakistan's biggest city stands within a few kilometres of the border of Baluchistan, the country's biggest province. The city has a population of six million living within an area of some 780 square kilometres; the province extends to 342,505 square kilometres but has a population of barely four million. This startling anomaly is partly a comment on human preferences for, all over the world, urban populations are exploding while numbers in the rural areas grow much more slowly as a result of out-migration. But the imbalance in Baluchistan is also due to the extremely tough environment which has, for centuries, imposed strict limitations on economic activity and, over vast areas of territory, allowed none but the hardiest of nomads to survive. Only in recent years has this picture begun to change with the development of the province's plentiful mineral resources. About 70 per cent of all the coal now mined in Pakistan comes from Baluchistan and the reserves of natural gas here are among the largest in the world. Gas from the Sui field is piped to Karachi, Hyderabad, Sukkur, Multan, Lahore and Rawalpindi, where it is used to power some of the nation's new industries. Baluchistan is also rich in chromite, marble, sulphur and iron ore.

The province takes its name from one of its three principal ethnic groups, the Baluch, although the Pathans and Brahuis are equally numerous.

The Pashtu-speaking peoples of Baluchistan are to be found concentrated exclusively in the relatively fertile hills and valleys to the

north and north-east of Quetta, the provincial capital. From there they continue northwards in an unbroken chain through the tribal belt of the frontier to Peshawar and beyond.

The Brahui and Baluch make their homes in the vast upland deserts stretching southwards and westwards from Quetta to the Arabian Sea. The Baluch claim an ancient Semitic lineage and trace their origins back over 4,000 years to Aleppo in Syria from whence, they claim, they migrated slowly eastwards. The Brahuis, by contrast, believe that they are indigenous to Baluchistan. This belief is supported by studies of their language which show it to be related to the ancient aboriginal tongues of the subcontinent that were largely displaced by the invading Sanskrit-speaking Aryans about 3,500 years ago. Both the Baluch and

Opposite: Gadiani Beach, about 40 kilometres west of Karachi. A heavy fishing boat is dragged ashore on log runners.

Right: Among Baluchi fishing families children learn the skills early in life and everyone lends a hand with the day's work.

Overleaf: Baluchi fishermen dry and clean their nets along the Makran coast to the west of Karachi, where fishing is an important industry.

Left: Fishermen with catch on lonely beach at Gwadar on Pakistan's Makran Coast, near the border with Iran. The waters of the Arabian Sea are rich with fish, and fishing is an important source of food and income for many in the south.

Opposite: Fishermen set off to check the day's catch in simple sailing canoe on coastal waters near Karachi.

Overleaf: Karachi's Clifton Beach at sunset, as the crowds begin to thin out and the beach takes on a soft romantic glow. In the background ships queue to off-load cargo in Karachi's busy harbour.

the Brahui are predominantly pastoral nomads, breeding sheep, goats and cattle and transporting their belongings on the backs of huge burden-camels as they move from place to place with their herds in search of pasture.

A fourth and distinct ethnic group in Baluchistan has recently received considerable attention from anthropologists. The Makranis, so-called because they inhabit the province's sere Makran coast that stretches from Karachi to the border of Iran, have pronouncedly Negroid/Hamitic features and closely resemble the people of the Horn of Africa. The Makranis are a fishing community and one folk-tale about

Left: An ancient steam train chugs slowly through the Bolan Pass. The railway was built by the British to open the strategic route between Afghanistan and the heartlands of the subcontinent.

their origin says that their ancestors were fishermen from Ethiopia who were blown far off course by a storm and ended up in Baluchistan. Another, more credible, theory is that the Makranis are descended from slaves brought to the subcontinent hundreds of years ago by Arab merchants; but this does not explain their concentration in Baluchistan. A third suggestion is that they are related to the ancient Indus Valley peoples of Harappa and Moenjodaro, who are thought to have had cultural and commercial links with Pharaonic Egypt.

Whatever the true explanation may be, there is no doubt that Baluchistan's Makran coast has a long and intriguing history. Alexander the Great led part of his army out of the subcontinent by way of Makran, and one thousand years later Mohamed Bin Qasim led his soldiers from Baghdad to Sind through Makran. Mohamed Bin Qasim was not dismayed by a reconnaissance report that described his chosen coastal route as 'a desert without any vegetation. . . . Water is scarce and the fruits not to the Arab taste. There are innumerable thieves and *dacoits*. If the army is small it will be wiped out and if large it will starve.' Mohamed Bin Qasim's expeditionary force was inspired by the fire of Islam, at that time a religion not one hundred years old, and made short shrift of the fierce Baluchi brigands who poured down out of the Makran mountains in attempts to impede the march. Much later, in the sixteenth century, the same turbanned tribesmen stood against the Mughal empire under Akbar and, indeed, remained free of any outside control for another 200 years. Though they bowed nominally to the British Raj, several bloody uprisings took place here between 1898 and 1901.

The British first came in force to Baluchistan in the late 1830s, during their campaign to install a monarch of their choice, Shah Suja, on the throne of Afghanistan. Britain's interest in these parts stemmed from her concern to contain Russian expansion into central and southern Asia. Afghanistan was viewed as an essential buffer-zone and neighbouring Baluchistan therefore took on great strategic importance.

In 1839 a British army marched up the Bolan Pass that links the Afghan border with Sind by way of Quetta. The columns were harassed by snipers all the way along the route, despite what had seemed like cast-iron guarantees of safe passage from the most influential local leader, Mir Mehrab, the Khan of Kalat. Subsequent evidence showed that the attacks in the Bolan had been instigated by the Khan's Chief Minister Muhammad Hussain, and that the Khan himself was not involved. The British, however, were looking for an excuse to extend their control over Baluchistan, so they seized their opportunity and launched an attack on Kalat saying that 'The conduct of the Khan was so treacherous, hostile and dangerous, as to require the exaction of retribution from that chieftain.' The retribution was swift and brutal. For two days in November 1839 the mud walls of the Khan's fort were

Overleaf: The town of Kulpur at the northern entrance to the Bolan Pass is an important railway terminus of Baluchistan. Coal mined in the Pass is freighted aboard trains to the nation's industries in Karachi and Lahore.

pounded to dust by shells from horse-artillery guns. In the hand-to-hand fighting that followed, the Khan was killed and the town seized.

A period of disorder marked by vicious internecine strife followed Mehrab's untimely death. For more than twenty years the Khans who succeeded him failed to get a grip on the country and the wild tribesmen who lived in it, despite the co-operation of the British. As one contemporary British observer wrote, 'The Baluch raided the Khan's country and made the Bolan Pass impassable, save by large caravans. So widespread and destructive were the raids that the Khan, assisted by our Resident, overran their country in 1859. For a moment the tribes were repressed, but not for long. Fierce disputes broke out between the Khan and his chiefs. He was deposed in 1863 and restored in 1864. Anarchy continued. The Khan employed a force of mercenaries, mostly Pathans. He fought with his chiefs with varying success, capturing some and then pardoning them; defied and resisted by others. The Bolan Pass remained quite unsafe, and other ways were closed altogether.'

Because of their interests in Afghanistan, the British regarded the Bolan Pass as an essential thoroughfare and it was therefore important to them to find some way to keep it open. If military force alone would not do the trick then they must find some way to come to terms with the tribes. A young officer, Robert Sandeman (later Sir Robert), was to play a key rôle in doing just this; in January 1876 he visited Kalat and became friendly with the Khan, although he disagreed with the ruler's forcibly expressed view that it was 'impossible to govern this country without a sword'. Sandeman returned in June of the same year, charged with the task of making peace between the Khan and the tribes. By a mixture of straight talking, tact and diplomacy he managed to do this. In the process he won the respect and affection of all concerned.

Sandeman, now the supreme British authority in Baluchistan, moved his headquarters to Quetta, leased the Quetta Valley from the Khan, and set about the task of keeping the surrounding countryside quiet and preserving its goodwill during the series of wars that Britain was to fight in Afghanistan. In this he was again successful. He used friendly conciliation rather than force wherever possible, and built up his alliance with the Khan. In 1881, while Sandeman was on a visit to England, the Khan wrote to him, 'I pray you to think of the sincere friend who is ever with you, like a second kernel in one almond.' For the next ten years, Sandeman travelled far and wide in Baluchistan, laying down the infrastructure of a peaceful administration and building for himself a reputation that has survived the passing of time. He died in the little southern town of Las Bela, worn out by overwork and exposure, on 29 January 1892. His last words, reputedly, were

Opposite: Sandeman Tangi, near Ziarat, is named after Sir Robert Sandeman, who headed the British military presence in Baluchistan during the 1880s. Tangis, long, narrow clefts in mountainsides and cliff faces, a feature of the countryside around Quetta and Ziarat, are caused by earthquakes, to which this region is particularly prone. Tangis sometimes link one valley to another through several miles of sheer rock. Sandeman Tangi, however, is shorter than most, ending abruptly in a waterfall that pours down out of the heart of a mountain.

simply 'The Baluch people.' Sandeman was buried three days later, and a dome was built over his tomb by the Las Bela chief. The Khan of Kalat expressed profound grief when he heard of the death of his old friend. 'He should be buried,' said the Khan, 'either in his native home or in my dominions. If the Las Bela chief objects I am prepared to send an army and forcibly convey the body from his territory to Quetta.' Though this threat was not carried out, the way that the Khan expressed his feelings does show the unusual affection and regard that Sir Robert inspired.

Bela, Sandeman's last resting-place, is today a small market town on the north-south road that winds through the heart of Baluchistan from Karachi to Quetta. Just 145 kilometres from Karachi, something of the salty atmosphere of the coast still persists here. In the steep narrow streets of the market, all the tribal variety of Baluchistan is to be seen— fantastically turbanned Baluchis, lightly-veiled Brahui women in long, red dust-covered dresses, fierce-looking Pathan truck-drivers pausing for refreshment on their way north, and Makrani stall-owners in long, blue flowing robes.

Bela is surrounded by date palms and green, well-irrigated fields. Northwards, however, the road projects into a mountainous, stony desert that is endless in its vistas and harsh in its moods under the merciless indifference of a powder-blue sky. Here peasants scratch a living from the dusty ochre of the soil around occasional oases. These people are, for the most part, tenant-farmers, surrendering three-quarters of their produce to a landlord, who is also their tribal chief, in exchange for a little seed and the right to plough the land. So deeply ingrained are traditions in these parts, and so solidly established the social order, that no peasant would think of changing the system that keeps him and his family in perpetual servitude.

The real aristocrats amongst the Brahui-speaking peoples of Baluchistan are the nomads, who wander across the face of the desert without fear or favour following their camels and ragged flocks of sheep and goats. They move in fairly small groups, often just one man, his wives and a handful of children. In the early morning, their backs to the rising sun, it is a stirring sight to see these elemental communities commence their day's journey, the tall bearded patriarchs taking the lead with long firm strides, and the women following behind, goading on the heavily-laden camels with high-pitched commands. To the rear of the column, three or four trim and savage dogs nip at the legs of the heavily-fleeced fat-tailed sheep that are the nomads' principal source of wealth. Wooden camel-bells knock out a hollow rhythm, and the walkers cast long shadows.

Through Baluchistan, the road goes on and on, seemingly without end. In places it runs in a straight line for eighty kilometres or more. The country here, away from the Makran coast, consists of flat plateaux interspersed with mountain ridges that rise above the plains like the

vertebrae of giant dinosaurs long ago interred but now exposed by the withering elements. The soil is sandy, covered over with a loose layer of scrub vegetation. People, animals, plants and earth all seem to have been reduced by the pitiless sun to the colour of uniform khaki. Strong centrifugal winds create huge spirals of dust, a natural phenomenon that has, over the centuries, been the source of many chilling rumours of jinn summoned out from the core of the earth to haunt the sleep of superstitious desert-dwellers.

A day's drive to the north of Karachi, the small town of Khuzdar nestles amongst a knot of mountains—the confluence of the Krithar, Pab, Hala, Makran, Siahan and Central Brahui ranges. The valley floor here is about 5,000 feet (1,520 metres) above sea-level, the highest peaks about 10,000 feet (3,050 metres). The terrain is rugged and unforgiving yet, as the night falls over Khuzdar, the contours of the hillsides take on a softer, more rounded and friendlier glow. The moon rises in a clear blue sky of pulsating stars, and a breeze blows in off the plains purged of the heat of the day.

Khuzdar may lack historical distinction, but it holds the future in its hands. Huge reserves of good-quality iron-ore have been found and the workers required by the mines have flocked to the town, swelling its population and bringing it new prosperity.

In Kalat, a day's journey to the north, the picture is quite different. Here the future seems uncertain and the present unremarkable, but the past is crowned with pageantry and honour. The traveller arriving in Kalat is at first hard-pressed to see in the town's low mud dwellings and poorly-stocked shops any signs that this was once the capital of a prosperous princely state. Yet faint echoes do remain. A red British pillar-box, its letter slot now blocked, brought here on the idiosyncratic whim of a long-dead Khan, stands incongruous and forlorn in the main street. And on a hill above the town the mud battlements of a once formidable fortress rise cracked and weatherbeaten in decayed grandeur.

Kalat's fall from prominence five centuries after its foundation was accompanied by a concomitant rise in the importance of Quetta. The drive from the capital of the one-time princely state to the provincial capital of modern Baluchistan takes about four hours through an area of increasingly dense habitation. Small mud and burnt-brick settlements dot the plain, alternating with the distinctive shelters of the nomadic Baluchis. These portable dwellings are formed by a number of long slender poles, bent and inverted towards each other, over which are placed tarpaulins fashioned from the coarse black fabric of camel-hair.

Nearing Quetta the narrow asphalt road climbs wearily over the shoulder of a single ridge of mountain at Lac Pass beneath the blank, blind gaze of an empty picket fort. To the south the desert stretches

Above: Grapes for sale in a Quetta street. The provincial capital of Baluchistan is surrounded by orchards and vineyards which provide many varieties of fruit.

Above: Sajji—whole leg of lamb skewered on a wooden spit and then barbecued beside an open fire—is the regional culinary speciality of Baluchistan. It is cooked in the early evening at open roadside stalls after being marinaded in salt for several hours.

away, baked dry in the merciless summer heat that often exceeds 50°C; to the north a green and pleasant valley meets the eye at an altitude of 5,500 feet (1,675 metres), holding forth the prospect of cooler climes and fresher air.

The Quetta Valley was not always so inviting. In 1877, when Sir Robert Sandeman first came to establish his headquarters here, the place was 'water-logged and unhealthy and the town long had an ill name'. One of Sandeman's officers wrote, 'Thieves and robbers infested it in those days. It was seldom that a night passed over our heads without the report of firearms, and often one would get out of bed through fear.'

Prior to the arrival of the British, Quetta had been more commonly

Below: Prospect Point, vantage point of the hills above Ziarat, below which the land suddenly drops thousands of feet, giving a panoramic view of valleys and mountains. The fragrance of pine trees fills the air and the calls of hunting birds add an atmosphere of poignancy.

known as Shal and amounted to little more than a collection of mud huts clustered around a mound topped by an old fort that was occupied by the Khan of Kalat's soldiers. The name Quetta, which the incoming administrators adopted, in fact derives from the Pashtu word *kot* which means 'fort'.

The British set about building a cantonment soon after their arrival in Quetta, just as they had done elsewhere along the frontier. As a result, the town quickly began to grow. In 1891 it had a population of 18,802 including the 7,500 residents of the cantonment; in 1901 the total population was 24,584, which rose to 33,922 in 1911 and to 49,001 in 1921. A decade later, in 1931, Quetta had more than 60,000 inhabitants, divided more or less equally between the town and the cantonment.

By 1935 Quetta was the largest garrison town in the subcontinent. Its mood, conditioned by the 12,000 soldiers who lived there with their families, was described by a contemporary observer as 'inbred, sporting, cheerful and not unkindly.' In May of that year the already burgeoning population had been substantially added to by holidaymakers come to escape the fierce summer heat of the Plains and everyone was looking forward to the month of June, always a delightful period in the Baluchistan highlands. At 3 a.m. on the morning of 31 May, however, a violent earthquake shook the town sending a surging shock wave roaring across the floor of this happy and unsuspecting valley. Quetta's brick and mortar houses collapsed and, in the space of just thirty seconds, more than 20,000 people lost their lives.

The scale of the tragedy was really too large to comprehend. It passed beyond the normal realm of human experience and engendered an awesome fatalism in many who survived it. 'Men and women,' wrote one witness, 'did not live or die, or escape or sustain injury because of what they did or did not do. They were the playthings of the dragon under the earth. A twist of its tail this way or that, or an angry snort, saved their lives or sent them plunging to eternity.'

The earthquake was an unusual one. The focus of the greatest shock was long and comparatively narrow, with the result that the disruption experienced on either side of the main area diminished with extraordinary rapidity. Soldiers sleeping in quarters only three kilometres from the section of town in which the greatest damage occurred were unaware that anything untoward had happened until they were hauled out of their beds the next morning to help in the relief operations.

One British battalion of 700 men pulled 867 people alive from the crumbling ruins of the city, as well as 1,178 dead. One surgeon, working around the clock, conducted 159 major operations in four days. Some 10,000 casualties were treated in the hastily-erected field hospitals and more than 4,000 patients were detained for observation.

Determined that no such disaster should ever again occur on the same scale, Quetta's administrators called in architects, engineers and designers to replan the city completely. Many streets were widened as a result, and a building code was introduced that stipulated earthquake-resistant structures.

The city that stands today is a product of the 1935 plan. The main thoroughfare is Jinnah Road, while the parallel Shahrah-e-Pehlavi is a long, broad boulevard lined with plane trees. In the Kandahari and Liaquat Bazaars tea-shops alternate with stalls selling local handicrafts like fine Baluchi mirror-work embroidery and green onyx carvings. The regional culinary speciality known as Sajji is also plentifully available, although not inexpensive. Sajji is a whole leg of lamb skewered on a wooden spit and then barbecued beside an open fire. Before cooking, the meat is marinaded in salt for two or three hours.

Quetta's bazaars offer a rich assortment of fresh fruit, including grapes, peaches and apples. The colourful orchards of the surrounding countryside give this part of Baluchistan a special charm, unique in Pakistan. The Urak Valley, about twenty-two kilometres from Quetta, seems bathed in eternal spring, with the green and russet hues of the apple trees offset by the pale blue of the sky. A small waterfall splashes down into an irrigation channel and Pathan farmers gather nearby to drink tea and pass the time of day.

Hanna Lake, eleven kilometres from Quetta, provides a contrasting form of beauty. Set amongst low brown hills, this picnic spot is popular with the townspeople of Quetta for its tranquil waters and cooling breezes. In the evening, as the sun slopes low in the sky, the lake takes on first a turquoise and then an emerald green colour, and the shrine set on the small island in its midst is cast in stark relief by the last light of the day.

About four hours' drive to the north-east of Quetta the little town of Ziarat stands amidst a forest of aromatic junipers at a height of 8,200 feet (2,500 metres). Here, during his last illness, Quaid-i-Azam Mohammad Ali Jinnah came to benefit from the clear, invigorating mountain air. The Quaid stayed far up on one of the green hillsides above Ziarat in a house built by the British in 1882 as the summer headquarters for the Agent of the Governor-General. The house, now known simply as the Residency, is one of those peaceful places in the world where the soul finds rest. It is surrounded by green lawns terraced into the contours of the hill and by bright, softly-scented flower

Opposite: Photographer at work with antiquated camera in the streets of Chaman—a town on the border between Pakistan and Afghanistan at the end of the Khojak Pass. Pathan men enjoy posing for pictures.

gardens. The overarching *chinar* trees cast patches of cool, deep shadow dappled with sunlight and, in the stillness of the morning, voices from the town below carry faintly, contributing to the intangible magic of the moment.

Walking in the gardens, and in the high empty hallways and shady curtained rooms of the old house, you are overtaken by a sense of awe and grandeur. Something of the spiritual quality of the great man who spent his last days here survives in the fabric of the place, a gentle, sympathetic, intelligent presence that the passing of time will not banish, nor the changing world erase. Toti Khan, the *chowkidar* who served here during the week before the dying Quaid was rushed by road to Quetta and thence by air to his residence in Karachi, still tends the gardens and guards the gate. The father of the nation, he says simply, 'was a very kind-hearted person. He used to talk to me. He liked to be surrounded by ordinary people.'

The countryside around Ziarat is filled with dramatic beauty. At Prospect Point, 8,900 feet (2,712 metres) above sea-level, the land drops away suddenly into a vast natural amphitheatre filled with pines. Hunting birds soar effortlessly on the thermals and their high piercing calls echo across the valley in the crystal purity of the Alpine air. This landscape, subject for millennia to the violent forces of earthquakes, is riven by gullies and empty watercourses. In places whole hillsides have been split open as though by blows from the edge of some giant hand. These defiles, or *tangis* as they are called, sometimes link one valley to the next through several kilometres of sheer cliff. At Chutair Tangi, about thirteen kilometres from Ziarat, the passage-way is so narrow that the sky is completely obscured, and falling boulders are trapped on their downward journey by jutting ledges of rock. The nearby Sandeman Tangi, named after Sir Robert, who loved to wander in these hills, is a cool grotto ending abruptly where a waterfall cascades out of the dark heart of a mountain.

The tendency of the earth to split and divide, which opened up the *tangis* north of Quetta, also produced the wider and more historic thoroughfares that gave the town prominence at the end of the last century. Running southwards and eastwards, the massive Bolan Pass cuts for eighty kilometres through the heart of the Central Brahui Range to the town of Sibi and to the province of Sind beyond. To the north and west, the steep and winding Khojak Pass gives access to Afghanistan through a spur of the Toba Kakar Range.

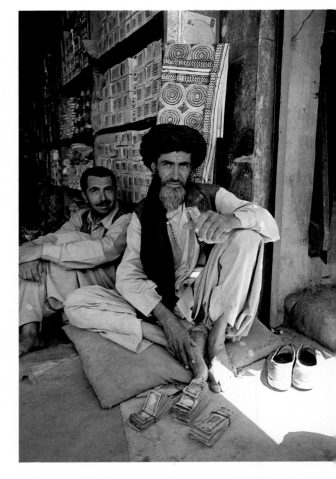

Above: Baluchi money-changer with piles of Afghan and Pakistani rupees in the streets of Chaman.

Above: A tea-stall at Chaman. The use of small individual teapots is unique to the frontier areas.

Overleaf: Arid, burnt out landscape marks Khojak Pass, the winding gateway between Pakistan and Afghanistan which straddles a range of hills north of Quetta.

The nineteenth-century British 'forward policy' aimed at the containment of Russia depended heavily on the government's ability to move troops quickly and efficiently through these passes from Punjab and Sind to the Afghan border. Driving through the Bolan Pass today it is not difficult to envisage the manner in which the local tribes harassed the heavily-laden columns of soldiers. The steep hills above the narrow road provide ideal cover for snipers and ambushers while the frequent tunnels through which the railway track passes offer many hiding-places for high-explosive charges and must have been extremely difficult to guard.

The terrain of the Bolan is rugged, dusty and dry. Here, each winter, thousands of wandering nomads with their massed herds of cattle, camels and sheep, make their way from the mountains of Afghanistan to the warm plains of central Pakistan. When summer comes they return to the fresh green grazing grounds of the hills. At times as many as a thousand camels can be seen gathered round the date palms and lush vegetation of the Bolan's infrequent oases, while the tents and skin-shelters of the nomads extend for miles in all directions along the stone-strewn floor of the Pass. The town of Mach, mid-way between Quetta and Sibi, is a melting-pot of travellers and merchants from all parts of the country, and also home to a large force of migrant labourers come to dig out the coal that has recently been discovered here.

The railway that runs up from Sukkur and Sibi through the Bolan Pass to Quetta continues north-westwards, cutting its way in a long tunnel through the final range of mountains that divide Pakistan and Afghanistan. The Khojak Pass carries the parallel ribbon of road across precipitous drops and around a series of acutely-angled hairpin bends. To rest the eyes of the weary traveller a vast panorama unfolds from Khojak Top through the wide vee of the descending hills into the limitless red plains of Afghanistan beyond. Here, at the border town of Chaman, amongst vivid bazaars and broad and dusty streets thronging with all the irrepressible life of the frontier, our journey through Pakistan, begun so long ago not many kilometres away in the Khyber Pass, comes to a fitting end.

It has been a journey through extremes of climate, from the snows of the far north to the searing heat of the south and west, and a journey through a mosaic of dramatic physical contrasts: mountains and plains; rivers and sea; rich and fertile valleys and hostile and barren deserts. It has also been a journey through many cultures, involving an attempt to understand their ultimate unity in Islam and in nationalism. In another sense, it has been a journey through history, for here the very ancient and the very modern co-exist as they do nowhere else in the world. Finally, and most importantly, there has been an inward journey too, in the sense that getting to know other people and other lands enhances our knowledge of ourselves. The people of Pakistan, Dr Muhammad Iqbal's 'compatriots to the whole world', have been sympathetic, engaging and gentle companions.

Opposite: Midday sun gives a diamond-like quality to the many facets of a waterfall crashing down a sheer rock face.